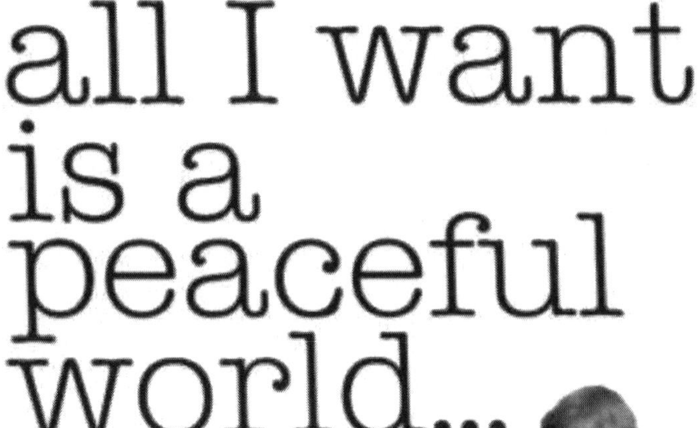

Ray Evans,
age 8.
Building a life
after the Blitz!

Ray Evans

Published by Ray Evans

1st Edition License Notes

To protect the privacy of individuals mentioned in this book, the names of many people and places may have been changed.

Every effort has been made to fulfil requirements with regard to reproducing copyright material. The author and publisher will be glad to rectify any omissions at the earliest opportunity.

ISBN-13: 978-1493799374 Paperback
ISBN-10: 1493799371 Paperback

Cover Design | Layout | Formatting
by WP-WebWorks.com

For Teresa,
with Best wishes
Ray Evans

all I want is a peaceful world and a pork pie!

What Others Are Saying...

I read this book to my elderly Mother, we were both riveted from the start! I found the stories gave me an 'escape' from the stresses in my own life and helped me appreciate that we all struggle in different ways but those who stay the course win in more ways than we could ever hope to.

My father fought in WW2 and lived through a similar period to Ray. But I never got a chance to talk to him about this period in his life. I actually feel that the author has opened up some of my own history and made it available to me. Can't thank him enough.

~ Elizabeth Jamieson – Devon UK

I'm not much of a reader but I blasted through this book in four days. It's an easy, fast enjoyable read. I'm looking forward to following your blog posts!

~ Tom Norman – NB Canada

I read "Before The Last All Clear" a couple of years ago and was desperate to know what happened next. I'm very happy to say I found this book just as easy to read and equally as hard to put down! Well done Ray and thank you for sharing your life stories with all of us not just your family.

~ Lola Santos – Florida USA

After reading Ray's first book I was looking forward to finding out what happened to him upon his return to Liverpool. "All I Want Is A Peaceful World and a Pork Pie!" didn't disappoint! It was a really quick read, basically because I couldn't put it down. I have always loved history as told through the lives of the people who lived it! Ray tells his story with warmth and humor, from the perspective of a regular guy trying to navigate an uncertain future. Ray, like his country, has been knocked down but his spirit is stronger for the experience. The courageous, mischievous little boy in "Before The Last All Clear" grew into a self-reliant, innovative young husband and father.

~ Cindy Lee – Virginia USA

"All I Want Is A Peaceful World...and a Pork Pie!" is the perfect sequel to Mr. Evans's first book, "Before the Last All Clear". The story picks up with the family reuniting and learning to live together again. Just as we learned of Ray's strength and determination to survive in his first book, that determination follows him through life in his many adventures as an entrepreneur and provider. The story easily guides the reader through the remainder of Ray's childhood, into his young adult life and finally into family-hood; many times with both ups and downs, but always with that never ending determination. He's a true inspiration and I am once again honored to have had the chance to read his story.

~ Pamela Kosmowski – Virginia USA

all I want is a peaceful world and a pork pie!

Acknowledgments

To Lilian, for putting up with me for spending all those long hours buried in the basement office.

To all my family, (especially my siblings who've passed since the first book was published) for giving me plenty to be thankful for, the best and funniest stories, the memories and the moments that warm my heart just to recall them, which I'm sure they'd be quick to remind me...I'm not so good at, these days.

To my Welsh family, who welcomed me into their home, especially Mrs. Williams for rescuing me from the brink of falling into bad habits and bad company. For bringing me back to the right side of things with her unconditional acceptance, caring, love and encouragement.

To Mary Jo & Mike Hartnett, Mike for his sage writing advice and help with the back cover copy, both Mike & MJ for their boundless encouragement in regard to this and the first book too, and most of all for their much valued friendship.

Alex Lyth, for creating the REA logo and his work helping Debbie with the cover design.

To Debbie, for editing | formatting | layout | cover design | production and marketing for both print & electronic versions. Most authors have to spend a fortune and enlist an entire team to do all that she does for me through WP-WebWorks, and fortunately she is multi-talented much like myself☺! We've both endured the many challenges of her teaching me the computer, the many resulting "Id10t" errors (as she calls them) and also for introducing me to and teaching me "The Twitter". Next stop, world domination on Facebook, LinkedIn and Pinterest... whatever that means!

"Life isn't about how to survive the storm,

it's about learning how to *dance* in the rain."

Vivian Greene

*****

Evacuation makes you grow up – quickly.

My six years in exile taught me two things.

First to always look on the bright side, and secondly, to have the stamina not to allow the lows in life to get the better of me.

There's always a light at the end of the tunnel - you just have to look for it.

Ray Evans

For Lilian.

My dear wife, who has an inexhaustible inner light that glows in her darkest moments.

Table of Contents:

Images:

Images are the authors own unless otherwise noted.

Several images from Egypt permission to use courtesy of:

SuezCanalZone.com
SuezVeteransAssociation.org.uk
StaneyBriggs.com

About The Author:

Glossary:

All I WANT IS A PEACEFUL WORLD

and

A PORK PIE!

By

Ray Evans

The Evans Family
George John Evans
B 1901 - D 1966
Beatrice Marion Poingdestre
B 1903 - D 1965
George Earnest
B 1926 - D 1980
Elsie
B 1928 - D 2005
Francis Reginald
B 1929 - D 2013
Muriel
B 1931 - D 2013
Albert
B 1932 - D 1998
Raymond
B 1933
Stanley Richard
B 1935
Dorothy
B 1937 - D 2010
Edith
B 1939
David
B 1944

It's All Over

Dateline: September 1944.

The danger from Britain's skies had begun to subside bringing the years of horror and destruction to an end. There were now at last definite signs that peace was finally in sight. One in particular was 'half lighting' which was being allowed in people's homes. This meant (as long as you remembered to keep your curtains closed after dark) you were allowed to take your blackout sheets down from your windows. Even the cinemas and pubs were allowed to dispense with their blackout screens. Better street lighting (except for near the coast) was also allowed providing it could be turned off in case of a sudden air raid. Union Jacks and bunting were on sale in the shops and city stores. One of the most positive signs was the Government's decision to set in motion the return of all evacuated children back to their own families and homes. The slow progress back to normality and peacetime freedom had finally begun, convincing the people of Britain that the war could possibly be over as early as Christmas.

There was however a new problem on the horizon and that was a distinct shortage of housing. Although the evacuation process would be much easier to execute in reverse, the thousands of young people that had begun pouring back into the inner cities every day would create a serious housing problem for the government. Over three million properties had been destroyed by the bombings, so the recently almost empty cities were soon bursting at the seams. Those who were sent away under the evacuation scheme at the beginning of the war and did not have a home to return to would have to continue living in their billets until the authorities were able to re-house them. Only the families that had made private arrangements (which usually meant moving in with relatives or friends) were allowed to return. There was even talk of large numbers of evacuees still living with their surrogate parents long after the war had ended. Seven more months would pass by before we were able to return home.

North John Street, Liverpool City Center.
(Image source unknown).
Most of the city looked like this when we returned from South Wales at the end of the war.

Dateline: Monday, April 16th, 1945.

It's around four o'clock in the afternoon and as usual I'm first to arrive home from school. I enter the house by way of the kitchen just like always expecting to see Auntie busy preparing the evening meal. Only this time she's not there. She's not in the kitchen and the table's not even set. What's going on? Where could she be? She's always in the kitchen at this time of day. I hang up my school things in the hall, and before checking upstairs, I pop my head around the living-room door to check if she's in there.

"I'm over here," she says, in a broken voice, "in the arm chair."

I switch on the light and there she is, sitting in front of the fire with her hands wrapped around the empty teacup she's got resting on her knee.

"Is there something wrong Auntie? Why are you looking so sad?"

"Your Mother was here today," she says.

"She arrived shortly after you left for school this morning."

"What did she want?

She came to tell me you'll be leaving very soon to go back home to Liverpool."

"But where are we going live? I thought our house got bombed?"

"I don't know, Raymond, she never said."

For a brief moment it seems impossible to believe the words that are coming out of my foster mother's mouth. I've been waiting for this day to arrive for close on six years and now suddenly, without any warning whatsoever, it's here; it has finally arrived.

"When Auntie? When do we leave?"

"Next Monday" she says, "on the morning train."

I make a beeline for the kitchen, grab the calendar from the wall, rush back in to the lounge and hold it in front of her.

"Look Auntie, just seven more days and I'll be going home. I've marked it on the calendar, see?"

She sets her cup and saucer down on the tiled hearth, leans forward and takes hold of my hands to pull me closer.

"Come closer," she says, "kneel down; I want to ask you something."

For a few seconds her silent gaze remains steady on my face, then in a throaty voice, she says:

"I'm going to miss you Raymond, we all are. You've become part of the family over these past two and a half years. Things just won't be the same without you."

The excitement and happiness of being told I'm going home has suddenly become tinged with the bitter understanding that I may be leaving here forever, that I might never see Auntie again. Great big tumbles of emotion begin to stir up inside me. She wipes her eyes with her tiny lace handkerchief, puts her arms around me, and in her soft lilting Welsh accent, says:

> "Your evacuation days are over Raymond; this terrible war is finally coming to an end."

The inability to put words to all the conflicting emotions I am now feeling make it impossible to speak.

> "I know Liverpool is a long, long way from here," she says, "but I want you to make me a promise, a solemn promise that is. I want you to promise me that you'll come back and see me one day."
>
> "I will Auntie, I promise"

Leaving Llanelli

It wasn't until those last few days in Llanelli, realizing my return to Liverpool was now imminent, that I began paying more attention to the newspapers. Up until then, just like most 12 year olds, I was more into comics. Interested only in what Desperate Dan and Laurel & Hardy were getting up to. I became hyper-aware of the horrific images and devastation that had been wrought across our small country for so many years. When I read the articles from beginning to the end, sometimes twice over, the stories and images I found so shocking now began to haunt me in my sleep.

Broken dreams kept waking me at night until it became impossible to get back to sleep. I kept dreaming the same dream over and over again. Dreaming I was back in Liverpool walking along the bombed-out streets with my mother and brothers and sisters searching for our house in Brookbridge Road. Everywhere was a scene of utter devastation, bombed out houses shops and even churches, everywhere I looked. Parents and children rooting through the wreckage of their bombed out homes searching for anything they could find.

I wake yet again and lay staring into the darkness trying to erase those horrible dreams out of my mind; trying to remember what Liverpool really looked like before I was evacuated, before all the bombings.

But no matter how hard I try, the memories of those days have all but faded into the past. It's as though I'm left with a big hole in my memory. Five and a half years have washed away practically all traces of life before the war. The only picture that still lingers in the back of my mind is of the actual day I'm leaving, my very last day at home, evacuation day, September 4th, 1939.

In my memory of that day, I'm sitting on the drain-board in the kitchen looking into my mother's eyes as she wraps the bandage around a deep cut on my forehead. She has a sad and anxious look about her, the kind I've never seen before.

"Is there something wrong Mum, are you worried about something?"

"No, she says, nervously, "there's nothing wrong son, it's just that I have a lot to do today."

"Where are we going?"

"You're going on a nice long train ride today. Isn't that nice?"

"Oh great, I've never been on a train before. Where are we going to?"

"I'll not be coming with you, not right away, but I will be following on later."

"Why later? Why not now? You will be coming with us won't you?"

"I can't right now, I've just told you. I've got a lot to do."

"But Mum, you still haven't told me where we're going?"

"To the countryside, you'll like it there, lots of fields for you to play in, lots of trees to climb."

I lay awake thinking how much the war has changed everything and everybody, how things are so different and not the same anymore. I'm thinking about the last time I visited my Mum in her billet; when she scolded me for not visiting more often. She kept telling me I'd changed and that I'd grown apart from everyone; that I acted like a stranger in the house. I remember her being very upset and very annoyed with me about that.

I think about the time when aunty first took me in, a day I know I'll remember as long as I live. It was a bright warm summer's day in the middle of June, 1943. I was only nine and a half years old, yet I'd already been bounced from billet to billet for close on three and a half years. The world I was forced to live in seemed to be in utter chaos. I remember the usual fear and anxiety creeping over me as my billeting officer led me down the street to my new billet. It would be my sixth move in a little over three years. It would've been much easier if I had known what I know now, that it would be my last "new home" before returning to my real home and family. The fear of not knowing what my new "foster parents" were going to be like was making my stomach turn over; just like it did each time I was moved to yet another billet. But it all disappeared in an instant the moment my new landlady, Mrs. Williams took my hand and welcomed me into her home. The kindness and love I was shown over the next two and a half years formed a bond so strong it would stay with me to this day. Mrs. Williams and her family opened a door to a new future for me on that day in 1943; a door I'm positive would have remained closed had I been taken to live with someone else.

That's me 2nd from the right with some of my pals, taken in Llanelli when I was about 8.

Two of my best pals, Eddie Thompson and Jack Cadwallader were already back in Liverpool. They left over a year ago. Poor Tommy Flint on the other hand (my other best mate) won't be coming with us because he died a few weeks ago after falling off the top of the old stone quarry where we used to play. No one knows exactly what happened because he was on his own when it happened. Some say it was suicide through missing his mother, convinced he would never see her again. I wonder if his Mum knows where he's buried and if anyone will think to put flowers on his grave if she doesn't. The most shocking thing was that Tommy was just coming up to his twelfth birthday just like me, except he'd never see it or his home ever again. I decided then, maybe I was lucky after all.

*****

After being taken around the street to say my last goodbyes to all the neighbors, Mrs. Williams escorts me to the station to meet up with the rest of my family who like me had been billeted in various houses in different parts of the town. Llanelli felt strangely quiet and empty that day, making me wonder if we were the last evacuees to leave.

I've forgotten how "grown up" I am supposed to be and begin to cry when the time comes to wish my foster mother farewell. I pick up my brand new suitcase Auntie bought for me and make my way over to the train to join the others who are already seated in the compartment. I'm the last to board the train which means the porter can now close the carriage doors and blow his whistle so the train can get on its way. It moves off almost immediately, puffing and squeaking its way out of Llanelli station out into the Welsh countryside, taking us on our long journey back to the war torn, bombed out-streets of Liverpool.

I pause in the corridor and press my face against the shuddering glass so I can wave to Auntie one more time. She's still on the seat where I left her, waving her tiny lace handkerchief. I keep waving back until I can't see her anymore, her last words ringing in my ears.

> "Don't forget your promise Raymond, you will come back and see me, won't you?"
>
> 'I will Auntie, I promise.

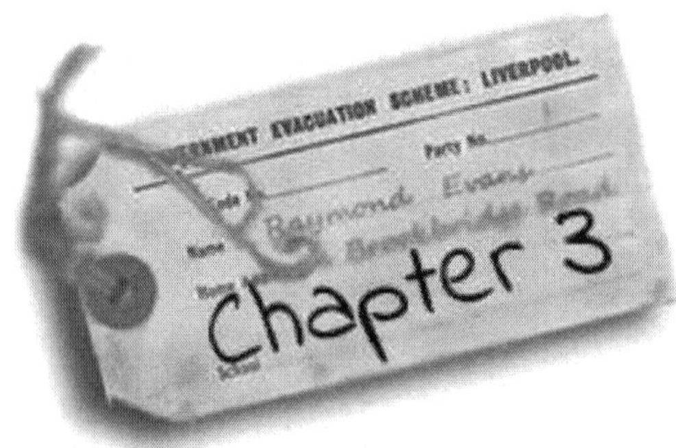

Return To Liverpool

Dateline: 30th April, 1945 Edge Hill Station, Liverpool.

We're lined up in the corridor behind my mother waiting for the porter to open the carriage door. She peers through the window hoping to catch sight of Grandma and Uncle Harold. But it's impossible to see them amongst the hordes of people that are now crammed on the steamy platform; children, parents, relatives and lots of men in uniform.

"Maybe they're in the waiting room," my mother says, "come on, let's try there."

We push and shove our way across the platform to the 'Waiting Room' where Grandma and Uncle Harold are sitting in front of a roaring fire drinking tea. After lots of hugs and kisses, we pick up our cases and bags and join the stream of people making their way out of the station, Mum and Grandma talking ten to the dozen.

> "I'm sorry for keeping you waiting for so long," my Mother tells Grandma, "But we've been stopping and starting all day long picking up evacuees and soldiers. I thought we'd never get here."

> "Doesn't matter," Grandma says, "you're home at last and that's all that matters."

> "Where's Grandad?" Elsie asks. "Didn't he come with you?"

> "He doesn't like railway stations," Grandma says, "It's all the steam, gets on his chest and starts him coughing."

Uncle Harold, a smart slim self-assured man with wavy black hair, frowns and shakes his head in disbelief, wondering why his mother is always covering up for his father. Uncle Harold told me later if he'd had his way that day, he'd have told Elsie the truth and wouldn't have thought twice about it. He'd have told her that before leaving the house that morning, he and her Grandmother had begged and pleaded with Grandad to come to the station.

> "You haven't seen your Grandchildren for almost six years, for God's sake!" Grandma had said.

But like always, all the begging and pleading would not make one iota of difference to my Grandfather. His afternoon was going to be spent propping up the bar in the Kings Arms pub around the corner, and nothing, my Grandma said, was going to change his mind.

*****

Aunt Lucy's house was situated half way along Beaumont Street on the opposite side to her busy fish and chip shop, a business that has yielded her a good steady income over the past twenty years or more - even through the worst of the war years. The house was notably Victorian in origin having the typical high ceilings, elaborate moldings and large heavy wooden doors. The fancy iron railings that once outlined the perimeter of the property had long since disappeared. Aunt Lucy, like everyone else in Beaumont Street, had willingly donated the metal railings to the war effort to be melted down and used to build tanks and airplanes.

In the early twenties when Aunt Lucy's husband was alive and before the great depression laid its hands on the city, Beaumont Street was THE place to live – a place where wealthy and respected members of the community once dwelled, politicians, lawyers, ship owners and the like. Those who could afford to drive around in swanky petrol driven motor cars, an area once known as the 'posh' side of Liverpool, where people were able to afford butlers, maids and nannies.

Kathleen, Aunt Lucy's middle aged daughter, whom I can't remember too much about except that she came across as a little odd at times, was a small feeble little woman who always dressed in dark clothes and had the strange habit of stomping around the house in her "noisy" black laced boots singing 'Jesus loves me yes I know, 'cos the bible tells me so…nothing more, just those two lines over and over and over again! Actually, I don't think the poor woman was altogether with us. In fact, in the short time that I lived in Aunt Lucy's, I found out something about Kathleen that her mother knew nothing about. Nor did anyone else for that matter; and that was the secret passion she had for the local window cleaner who lived a few doors away. The little man had unwittingly enamored her by giving her a peck on the cheek each time she filled his bucket with clean warm water.

Kathleen was so besotted with this man. She didn't see him as the little dumpy bald headed person he really was; not in her eyes anyway. She saw him as being a tall dark handsome man, a Clarke Gable type you might say. So strong were her feelings towards this little fellow, she would often sneak out of the house to buy him expensive gifts, using the money she stole from the metal cash box her mother kept under her bed. It was always full to the brim with coinage she'd accumulated from the weekly chip-shop takings; half crowns, two shilling pieces, shillings, and lots and lots of pennies and halfpennies. There she was, flat out on her stomach halfway under the bed filling the pockets of her pinafore. I actually saw her with my own eyes. She bribed me with a whole shilling never to tell anyone. I never did.

*****

Because there weren't enough beds at Aunt Lucy's, it was decided that Frank and I would spend our nights at Grandma Evans's house. Frank did not in any way relish the idea of living with Grandad, not after all he'd been told about him, about his reputation of being grumpy all the time, of not wanting to speak to anyone; least of all his children.

"You'll only be sleeping at your Gran's," mum explained,

"You'll eat your meals here with us."

"How long do you think it'll be?" Frank asked. "I know Grandad won't like us staying there, even for one night."

"Two or three months at the most," my mother said, "That's all."

I'm sure she believed that at the time, and even if she didn't, I'm sure she hoped with all her heart that it would only be for a very short period. We'd been apart for the past six years and she must've been desperate to have the family back under one roof again.

"Just be sure to stay out of his way," she said, "that's all you need to do."

"What if I ask Grandad a question? He'll have to speak to me then, won't he Mum?"

"No, you're not to speak to your Grandad unless he speaks to you first. You'll upset him asking him questions every few minutes."

"But I wasn't going to ask him questions every few min..."

"You're always asking questions Raymond. You do it all the time. I've lost count how many questions you asked your Uncle Harold on our way home from the station.

Personal questions some of them were, it's just not right."

"But…"

"There are no buts about it. I don't want you upsetting him. He'll get annoyed and start bawling and shouting - do you understand?"

"Yes Mum."

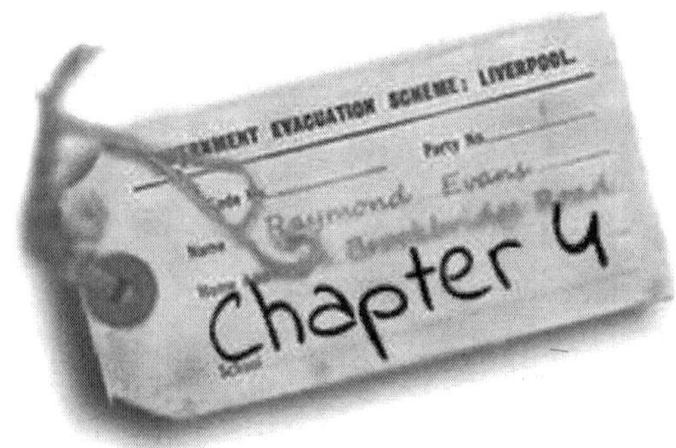

Rise And Shine

My mornings at Grandma's began at the crack of dawn just as it was breaking light. When the muted voices of Cam Street's early morning workers could be heard as they traipsed along the back alley below. When the lamp lighter could be heard tapping on our neighbor's bedroom window prompting Mrs. Devlin to shout her son Alfred to get up for work. Her loud "fog-horn" voice, I was sure, could be heard several streets away.

"ALFREEEED! DID YOU HEAR THAT? THE KNOCKER-UP MAN HAS JUST TAPPED ON THE WINDOW!

ARE YOU LISTENING TO ME ALFRED?

DID YOU HEAR WHAT I JUST SAID? THE KNOCKER-UP MAN HAS JUST BEEN, FOR GOD'S SAKE ALFREEEED!"

"I'M UP MUM. HONEST, I AM UP."

"NO YOU'RE NOT, YOU LYING LITTLE SOD, I'M NOT STUPID. I KNOW YOU'RE BANGING YOUR SHOE ON THE FLOOR."

"BUT I AM UP MUM."

"IT'S HALF PAST SIX! YOU'LL BE LATE FOR WORK...... AGAIN!"

People relied on the lamp lighter (or 'knocker-up man' as he was commonly known) for their early morning 'knock-up' calls which, for the princely sum of one or two shillings per week, was a service he would gladly provide by simply tapping lightly on your bedroom window with the long wooden pole he used to snuff out the flames of the street's gas lamps.

Frank and I slept in the tiny box room that over-looked the back yard and back alley. The old brass bed (once used by Uncle Harold) which was neither a single nor a double was sandwiched between a small narrow wardrobe (on my side of the bed) and a round glass topped table on Frank's side. The black metal fireplace set across the corner on the opposite wall a few feet to the left of the window, only got lit when there was an extra bag of coal to spare. Grandma could barely afford to keep the kitchen fire going never mind a fire in the bedroom.

Everyone 'backed' their fires up before going to bed in those days. Not only to keep the house warm overnight, but more importantly, to prevent the big fat lead water pipes from freezing up. A few large lumps of coal with a thick layer of slack usually did the trick. That would pretty well guarantee to keep the fire burning throughout the night, at least until the early hours of the morning anyway.

At seven o'clock or thereabouts, Grandad could be heard lighting up his first cigarette of the day, the one that made him cough his guts up even before he got his trousers on. I could never understand why my Grandad ever bothered to smoke, considering how much he suffered with his chest. He had one of those nasty rattling chesty coughs that seemed to come up from the soles of his boots.

There was one morning I remember when Frank (before leaving for work) came up to tell me Grandad had forgotten to back the fire up the night before.

> "I'd stay in bed a bit longer if I were you," Frank said, "at least until Grandad has got the fire going and the kitchen's warmed up. It's freezing and you can see your breath down there."
>
> "He was drunk again, Frank, that's why!"
>
> "How do you know that?"
>
> "Because I was awake and saw him stumbling into the yard - he was so drunk he could hardly stand up."
>
> "So you were up nosing through the window again?"
>
> "I wasn't nosing. I got up to see who it was coming into the back yard; it could have been a burglar - you never know."

"Well anyway, there's no school today, so you might as well stay in bed until the kitchen warms up, it's like an ice box down there."

"I don't want to stay in bed, Frank. I won't be able to get back to sleep, not now."

"Stay where you are and keep out of Grandad's way, he's not in a very good mood. He won't want to be listening to you bothering him with questions every few minutes, especially while he's trying to light the fire."

"But I'm hungry Frank."

"Hungry? You're always hungry. Just try doing as you're told for once? It's windy outside. He's having trouble lighting the fire and you know what he's like when he can't get the fire lit. It's guaranteed to put him in one of his really bad moods."

"Ok, but leave the bedroom door open then?"

"Why do you want the door left open?"

"So I can hear what's going on down stairs. So I know when to get up."

"What do you mean, so you know when to get up?"

"When I know the fire's lit and it's safe to go down there."

"How will you know when the fire's lit?"

"By listening for all the different noises and sounds coming up from the kitchen, I can even tell what stage he's at with lighting the fire. I do it every morning after you've gone to work; it helps pass the time."

"What noises? What sounds?"

"Well, for a start, the loud noise he makes rattling the fire grate with the poker. I bet even next door can hear that. It's enough to wake up the dead."

I wasn't sure what was going through Frank's mind but he smirked a little as he encouraged me to continue "Go on."

"Erm... let's see. Oh yes, I can hear him in the backyard emptying the ashes into the bin. In fact I can even hear him going down the cellar steps for a bucket of coal."

"But how do you know when he's actually got the fire lit if you're still in bed, that's what I'd like to know?"

"I haven't finished yet Frank. I'm getting to that."

"Hurry up. I've got to go to work don't forget. I don't believe that, you're just making it up. You can't hear him filling the coal bucket all the way down there."

"I didn't say I could hear him filling the coal bucket, I said I can hear him going down the cellar steps. And anyway, that's not all I can hear from up here. I can hear people talking outside, even when the window's shut. I can hear every word they're saying. In fact, if I open the bedroom window a little, I can hear people talking three houses away. I can even hear them flushing their toilets!"

"Three houses away? I don't believe you"

"Yes I can Frank, honest to God. These houses are so close together you can hear all sorts going on. I can even hear the man next door talking to his pigeons, and that's when he's inside his shed, not outside. He talks to those pigeons every morning before he leaves for work. Did you know he has names for every one of his pigeons, Frank? Like Joey, and Billy and Flash. I wonder how he can tell one from the other; have you ever thought about that? I don't know how he tells them apart. I think I'll ask him next time he's in the yard."

"You must have your head stuck out of the window to hear all that stuff going on, because I can never hear anything like that when I'm in bed."

"You're always fast asleep Frank, that's why."

"Ok, but you still haven't told me how you know when the fire's lit!"

"Well I've not got there yet Frank, Grandad's still in the cellar don't forget."

"For God's sake, does it really matter where he is? Just tell me how you know when the fire's lit."

"I can tell because I can hear the wood burning of course, you know how it makes those crackling and spitting noises."

"Well, just turn over and go back to sleep instead of listening for all these noises you keep going on about.

"But I just told you, I can't get back to sleep."

"You can't get back to sleep because you're too damn nosy, that's the top and bottom of it. Mum's right, you've always been nosy."

"I can't go back to sleep once I'm awake, Frank. I start getting hungry straight after I wake up. My stomach starts rumbling. It's rumbling right now, can't you hear it?"

"That doesn't surprise me, no wonder everyone calls you Porky!"

*****

It was long after Frank had left for work that day when I suddenly realized everything had gone unusually quiet down stairs. I'd been lying on my back for quite some time, my hands locked behind my head looking up at the ceiling thinking how nice it would be to be sitting in front of the warm fire sipping a cup of tea and munching on a nice thick slice of toast smothered with strawberry jam. There was nothing for it but to get up and find out what was going on down stairs. So I stretched over, grabbed my pants, vest, shirt and socks off the back of the chair and got dressed under the covers - just like I always did on very cold and frosty mornings. All that was left to do then was reach for my slippers before stepping out onto the ice cold linoleum.

Surely he's got the fire lit by now I thought to myself. Frank must've been gone over an hour. What's going on down there? As it was, I walked into a smoke filled icy cold kitchen to find my Grandad crouched in front of the fireplace still struggling to get the fire to light.

"Bloody wind," he was mumbling as he poked at the base of the fire, "Bloody wind keeps blowing the paper out."

Thinking it was me he was talking to I went over and knelt down beside him. The wind was blowing down the chimney like an express train.

"Are you having trouble lighting the fire this morning Grandad?"

"Mmmm."

"It's very windy this morning isn't it Grandad?"

"Mmmm."

"Making it very difficult to get the fire going?"

"Mmmm."

"Do you think it might rain today Grandad?" Looks very cloudy out there?"

"Mmmm."

It was no use; he acted as if he was deaf to everything I said. I stood up, grabbed my coat out of the hall, wrapped it around my shoulders and parked myself on the couch. The satisfied look on Grandad's face when he eventually got the fire to light, when the flames began reaching high up the chimney was well worth the wait. I thought for a moment this was going to be a special day, Grandad was actually smiling.

Thinking he was now in a better mood, I got up off the couch and knelt down beside him again. I was determined to give it one last try to get him to talk to me, to get him to at least say something.

"They're saying Hitler is not really dead Grandad; that he's escaped from his bunker in Berlin and no one has any idea where he could possibly be. Did you know about that Grandad? It's in all the papers."

"Mmmm."

"Does mmmm mean yes Grandad? Have you heard about that?"

"Mmmm."

It was no use; even the prospect of Hitler being alive failed to do the trick. He didn't even acknowledge I was in the same room as him. I looked up at the mantelpiece to check the time – seven o' clock. I still had an hour to wait before I was allowed to go over to Aunt Lucy's for my breakfast which meant there was nothing else to do but go back to sit on the couch and watch my Grandfather sit motionless in his lumpy armchair gazing distractedly into the fire. I can see him even now, looking so sad and forlorn sitting there with grandma's wooly hat perched on top of his head and uncle Alf's army overcoat draped over his shoulders.

*****

Grandma left for work dead on six every morning. I used to listen for her little footsteps along the back ally rushing to catch the bus. I felt so sorry for her having to go out to work at her age. House cleaners in those days were ten a penny and poorly paid at best. I asked her one day, why she chose to leave the house via the back door, not the front.

> "It's only in the winter I do that," she said, "when the cold weather makes the front door swell up."
>
> "I'm awake then Grandma," I said, "I could come down and open it for you."
>
> "Thank you son," she said, "that's nice of you, but forcing it will only make the knocker clack, and that's what wakes your Grandad up, the noise of the knocker clacking."

Wakes Grandad up? I was flabbergasted when she told me that. Why would she be so concerned about waking Grandad up when he was too lazy to go out to work himself? When he was even too lazy to get up in the mornings to make her a hot cup of tea before she went out to work?

> "But that's the kind of person your Grandma is," Uncle Harold told me one day. "A kind loving person who in all the years she's been married to your Grandad, has never once harbored any sour feelings towards him, or anyone else for that matter."

It's hard to figure out or even understand why my Grandmother put up with my Grandfather for so long. They had married in the spring of 1893, Uncle Harold had told me, when she was just seventeen years of age, a "mere slip of a girl" as he'd described her.

The only photo I ever saw of their wedding day was the one leaning against the clock in the middle of the sideboard. There was Grandad sitting comfortably in a big leather armchair looking like he was the Prime Minister of England. Grandma on the other hand, (who was standing to his side) had just a hint of a smile on her face. I asked Uncle Harold if he knew how long they'd been married.

"Work it out," he said, "they got married in 1893 and it's now 1945."

"Fifty two years" I said, "wow, that's a long time."

"Yes, he said, "and he's still treating her like she's his slave."

Divorce was seriously frowned upon in those days, nothing like it is now. It was something people didn't speak about. It was almost shameful, almost akin to committing a crime. How times have changed.

Electricity Is A Foreign Concept

I was sitting at the table one evening eating my supper listening to Uncle Harold trying very hard to talk Grandad into having an electric fire installed in the kitchen. Grandma was in the scullery making herself a cup of cocoa and filling her hot water bottle ready to take up to bed. Uncle Harold had tried on several occasions to talk his father into this, but just like always, my Grandad wasn't having any. The concept of an electric fire in the house didn't come easy to him. I listened to them arguing for well over an hour, long after Grandma and Frank had gone to bed. Uncle Harold getting more and more agitated with his pigheaded and obstinate father.

"Think about it, Dad," he said, "You won't have to be lugging heavy buckets of coal up those steep cellar steps anymore. It'll be much easier for you."

It's my house," Grandad said, raising his voice, "I pay the rent, which means I can do what I want!"

"But all you'll have to do is flick a switch." Uncle Harold said,

"It's as simple as that. No more messing with newspapers and bits of wood trying to get the damn fire to light. No more worrying where the money's coming from for the next bag of coal. The kitchen will be nice and warm for Mum when she's getting up and going out to work. Why don't you come over to my girlfriend's house sometime and see what I mean?"

"I don't care and I don't want to go over to your girlfriend's house," Grandad snapped,

"I'll not allow electric fires in this house, not while I'm alive, they're far too dangerous. And anyway, how am I supposed to make the toast without a proper fire? Go on, tell me that."

"With an electric toaster of course," Uncle Harold answered.

"And where's the money coming from for one of those? Certainly not out of my pocket if that's what you're thinking."

"I'll put the money up for an electric toaster" Uncle Harold said, "I've told you that before."

"Electricity's too expensive," Grandad said, "it's much more expensive than gas, we won't be able to afford it."

"Of course you'll be able to afford it," Uncle Harold replied angrily. "You'll be saving yourself a lot of money changing over to electricity. You'll save on coal, on firewood and on gas mantles."

"I'll think about it," Grandad said, "I'm going to bed."

"What is there to think about?" Uncle Harold said, thumping the table with his fist, "It's the right thing to do; even if it's just for Mum's sake. Go and ask him next door, he's just had electricity installed in his house."

"I don't need to ask him anything," Grandad replied, "It's none of his business."

"I know an electrician who works for the local council," Uncle Harold said, "He's a good friend of mine. He's willing to wire up the whole house for half the cost the council will charge, which I'm willing to pay for by the way, he told me so just the other day. It's dark and miserable in here, Dad. Electric lighting will be much better for Mum. I worry about her all the time. The house is always damp and cold; even in the summer."

"I'll think about it," Grandad said, "I'm going to bed.

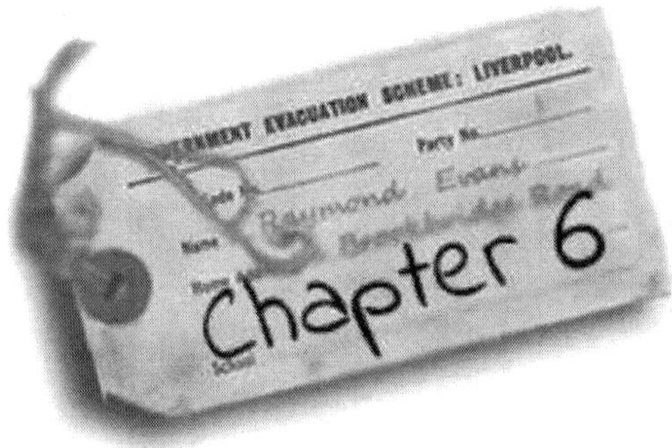

Uncle Harold Family Historian

Family history has always fascinated me. I was spellbound by the stories Uncle Harold told me, especially about my father in his younger days. Sometimes I got bits from my mother that Uncle Harold would piece together. His Saturday afternoon visits couldn't come around quick enough for me. I remember gazing out of the parlor window watching for him coming down the street.

> "Where were we up to?" he'd say, as he flopped down on the couch, "did you remember to make a note like I asked you to?"
>
> "Yes I did, Uncle Harold."

My most favourite story of all, was the one about my Dad getting his first job, and later, starting up his own little business a year later when he'd only just turned fifteen. Well, I'll let Uncle Harold tell it:

“It was your Uncle Bill, my eldest brother, the one with the gift of the gab, who talked Mr. Hawkins (the proprietor of Hawkins Dairies Ltd) into giving your Dad his very first job.”

‘How old was my Dad then?’

“That was the problem; our George had only just left school. He’d just turned fourteen, far too young for what Mr. Hawkins needed him for.”

‘So what happened?’

“Bill pleaded with Mr. Hawkins. He begged him to give young George a chance; suggesting he put him on a month’s trial to see how he turned out. George is a good lad, Bill told him; ‘he won’t let you down’.”

“What did Mr. Hawkins say; did he agree to give him a chance?”

“Yes he did. He put him with Ernie Crookshank, Mr. Hawkins’ longest serving employee. “Don’t let me down” your Uncle Bill told George when they arrived back at the house; “it’s taken a lot of persuading getting you this job, so you better work hard and don’t ever, ever, be late, Mr. Hawkins will sack you on the spot if you start coming in late. He hates people who can’t get themselves out of bed in the mornings.”

“What happened after that, did Mr. Hawkins keep my father on?”

“Yes he did, he did keep him on. As a matter of fact, Mr. Hawkins offered him a route of his own the following year, a week or so after his fifteenth birthday I think it was.”

“What about the firewood business Dad was supposed to be starting up, you said you’d tell me about that?”

“Oh yes, the firewood business, now that’s a story all of its own; you’ll have to wait until next Saturday to hear about that one. I’m not sleeping here tonight; I’m staying at my girlfriend’s house over the water.”

“Over the water? I don’t know what you mean.”

“She lives on the Wirral peninsula on the other side of the River Mersey so in Liverpool we call it ‘over the water’.”

“Where ‘over the water’ does she live?”

“In a little village called Irby.”

“How do you get there?”

“Either by car through the Mersey Tunnel, or on the ferry across the River Mersey.”

“Where’s the Mersey Tunnel?”

“You do ask a lot of questions Raymond. Tell you what, if you’re a good lad, maybe I’ll take you there next week on the bus. Sorry but I have to go now, the H8 only comes at five to and 25 past. I’ll see you next Saturday”

all I want is a peaceful world and a pork pie!

*****

One week later:

"So where did we leave off last week?"

"'You were about to start telling me about the firewood business when you had to rush off for the bus, remember?"

"Oh yes, I remember now."

"Well, it was one afternoon as George was giving the horse his nose-bag of oats when Ernie Crookshank came up to tell him Mr. Hawkins wanted to see him in his office right away."

"I'm very pleased with your work George, his boss told him. "I've been keeping a close eye on you this past year. You've not been late once since you started here, and that's very good. You're always first to clock in, I've been told. Plus, and this is a big plus, George, we've had good reports from your customers. So on the basis of that, I think you deserve a route of your own. I'm putting a lot of faith in you but I know you can do it."

"Which one Mr. Hawkins," George asked, excitedly, "which route are you thinking of giving me?"

"The route you're on now", his boss told him. "Mr. Crookshank is retiring. You can manage that can't you, George? You can manage a Pony and Trap on your own can't you?"

“Well our George couldn’t believe his ears”, Uncle Harold said as he went on telling me in great detail how this important and impactful event in my Dad’s life had come about.

“Oh yes Mr. Hawkins, I can easily manage the pony and trap. Mr. Crookshank used to let me take the rains sometimes. I can do it. No problem. Thank you very much sir.”

“Good,” Mr. Hawkins said. “That’s settled then. I’ll put you on a month’s trial to see how you get on. Any questions George?”

“Yes I do Mr. Hawkins,” George said, “What about my wages; will you be giving me a raise, will you be putting me on the same pay as Mr. Crookshank?”

“I don’t see why not,” Mr. Hawkins told him, “you’ll be doing the same job.”

“But what about the firewood businesses,” Uncle Harold, “you still haven’t mentioned anything about that?”

“I’m getting to that Raymond, don’t be so impatient; first things first.”

“Sorry.”

“Well it all took place about a year after your Dad got his promotion. It started one early morning when he was making his usual milk delivery to Morgan’s Bakery Shop in Lodge Lane, when he happened to notice Mr. Lambert the Greengrocer coming out of his store carrying a pile of empty orange crates. The idea didn't strike him right away; shop keepers were always dumping their rubbish in the alley, there was nowhere else to put it, you see."

"No bins?"

"Yes, of course there were bins. Everybody had a bin at the back of their shop. But they were kept for the normal everyday rubbish, not for the bigger things, like orange boxes, banana boxes, and fish boxes. Lodge Lane was a busy and bustling shopping area in those days; still is as a matter of fact, especially at the weekends. People round here have no need to go into town to do their shopping; they can get practically anything they want in the Lane, as long as they've got the money of course. I often wander down the Lane just for the pleasure of watching people go about their business. There are shops of every description from one end of the Lane to the other; at least fifty, if not more.

"Wow, that's a lot of shops."

"And that's not all. I nearly forgot about the swimming baths, the Library and the Pavilion Theatre. It's a very busy place is Lodge Lane. I wouldn't mind having a shop there myself. Anyway, enough of that, let's get back to the story. Now then, let me see, where was I?"

"Mr. Lambert the greengrocer was coming out of his shop carrying a pile of orange crates."

"Oh yes. It was when your Dad was climbing back up onto the milk float when the idea really hit him. Instead of moving off to his next call, he sat stock still for a few moments holding onto the reins staring down at the mound of orange, apple and banana crates heaped on top of each other in the alley. Excuse me Mr. Lambert," he shouted, "how much do you want for those wooden crates?"

"Nothing son," the Greengrocer answered, "You can have them for nothing, every last one of them. Actually, they're a nuisance; they're in the way. They clog up the alley."

"George couldn't believe his luck. He was sure he'd have to put his hand in his pocket and part with something, at least a penny or two for each crate. "I'll take them," he said, and all those others further down the alley, if that's ok with you, Mr. Lambert?"

"You can take what you want," Mr. Lambert told him; "they'll only finish up on the bin lorry."

"I'll not be able to pick them up 'till later this afternoon when I've finished my milk round. The wooden crates I mean, not the cardboard ones?"

"That's ok by me," Mr. Lambert said," but you'll have to make sure you're back here before the bin men arrive."

"What time do they get here?"

"Usually around three," Mr. Lambert said, "sometimes a bit before".

"I remember your Dad telling me, he had a hard time concentrating on his milk deliveries that morning. His mind kept drifting back to his little firewood business. It was all he could think about. Nothing else seemed important anymore. He'd even begun calculating how long it would take before he was able to give up his milk delivery job. To be his own boss and not have to take orders from that beaky-nosed smart-alecky little so and so Thelma Hawkins."

"Who's she?"

"The bosses' daughter, the person everyone disliked, including your Dad. In fact, George would have liked nothing better than to tell Thelma Hawkins to stick her rotten milk round where the sun…well never mind about that right now."

"What were you going to say?"

"Nothing, it's not important. I'll tell you another time. Let's get on with the story."

"OK."

I hated it when adults did that, leave you hanging in the air about to say something you're expecting to be really interesting then suddenly change their mind.

"The dislike he had for the boss's daughter wasn't just because of her squeaky irritating voice, it was the manner in which the cocky little so and so spoke to him when she was dishing out her orders, or when she was telling him to do something. Anyway, it was when he got to his last call, (Mancini's Italian Ice Cream Parlor in Wavertree Road) when he was halfway through his morning tea-break that it suddenly occurred to him. It hit him like a ton of bricks. How the heck was he going to get all those crates out of the side alley before the bin men arrived? He leapt up from his chair knocking it to the floor. How stupid he'd been not to think about it until now."

"What did he do?"

"He stood there for a few seconds totally bewildered. There must have been at least twenty five crates in the side alley that day; far too many for him to fit inside the old pram he was planning to use, the one his mother kept in the cubby-hole under the stairs. He had to find some other way of picking up crates before the bin men got there. Otherwise it could be the end of his little firewood business, there was absolutely no doubt about that. That would certainly put the kibosh on everything."

"What did he do?"

"Well, the first thing that flashed across his mind was the pony and trap. But that little brainstorm hung around inside his head for only a few seconds. It was absolutely forbidden for any employee to use the company's pony and trap for their own personal use. There were warning signs plastered all over the dairy walls."

> **"Any employee found using the pony and trap for their own personal use, will not only lose**

> **their job, but will forfeit part of their wages to go towards any wear and tear that the company thinks to be reasonable."**
>
> ***Signed: Thelma Hawkins... Daughter to the Proprietor.***

"The only alternative was for your Dad to hire a handcart. But how much was that going to cost? He dug his hands deep into his pockets and pulled out what was left from last week's pocket money - a shilling, a sixpence and three pennies, [1/9d] one shilling and nine pence."

"How much did he need?"

"I'll get to that in a minute, Ray, don't be so impatient."

"Sorry."

"It was two o'clock when he pulled into the dairy giving him barely an hour to stable the Pony, pick up the hand cart and get back to Lodge Lane before the bin men arrived. So, not sure whether he'd make it in time, he sprinted out of the dairy gates onto Smithdown Road and began racing up the hill towards Tunnel Road like he was taking part in some sprint race. The handcart hire was at the other end he'd been told, around the corner from the Tunnel Road Cinema. He was relieved when he turned the corner and saw in the distance the big wooden sign high above the door. Hand Carts for Hire – 1/3d per eight hour Day."

"So he did have enough money with him after all? He had sixpence left over, right?"

"Yes, you're right, which he was more than pleased about. But the problem now was, after giving the two-wheeled handcart a quick once-over, having had a good look at its thick wooden shafts and its heavy iron-clad wheels, George said he couldn't help feeling the handcart would need to be pulled by a horse, not a human being. The pushing and pulling up the hills and along the cobble stone streets was hard going even for a young fit sixteen year old. He could hear his heart thumping loud against his chest. But he did manage to make it back just in time before the bin men arrived. He was leaning against the cart getting his breath back after loading the crates onto the handcart when he saw the lorry turn the corner into Lodge Lane."

'How long did it take him to load the cart and get back to the house?'

"Not too long. Lodge Lane is only a few minutes' walk from Cam Street.

"What did Grandad say when he saw Dad carrying the crates into the backyard?"

"He wasn't there; he'd already left for the pub. But Mrs. Higgins the next door neighbour was - I do remember him telling me that. He said she was outside brushing her front step when she asked him what he intended doing with all the wooden crates. "I'm taking them around the back into the backyard,

Mrs. Higgins" your Dad told her, "I'm going to start up my own business selling firewood."

"Well bravo for you George?" she said "you can count on me being your very first customer. I spend a lot of money on firewood, especially in the winter, three to four bundles a week in fact. How much will you be selling yours for?"

"Tuppence a bundle, that's a ha'penny cheaper than Gorman's the chandlers sell theirs for, and I'll be delivering them right to your door."

"I'll spread the word around, George", she said, "Good luck to you, son!"

"Now this is where Michael O'Connor comes into the story."

"Michael O'Connor? Who's he?"

"Michael O'Connor was the street's principal gossipmonger, who while we're on the subject, just passed away a few weeks ago."

"What did he die of?"

"I don't know Raymond. I don't live around here anymore, do I? And anyway, what does it matter?

Why are you so interested in knowing what the man died of? It doesn't change the story."

"Sorry Uncle Harold, I just wondered that's all."

“He lived with his widowed mother in number twenty eight, a few doors down the street.”

“So he never got married then?”

“No son, he never got married.”

“What did he look like?”

“A big heavy built man with a mop of bright red curly hair - a man that spent most of his time getting to know everyone else’s business. In fact you couldn’t sneeze without Michael O’Connor knowing about it.”

“How old was he?”

“Hmm let me see, around forty five I think, maybe a little older.”

“Where did he work? What did he do?”

“If I remember right, he worked a five day week for the Parks and Gardens as a shovel and pick-man, the one and only job he ever had from leaving school, or so I believe. He was a strange odd sort of person. He spent most of his weekends sitting on the front step with a blanket wrapped around his shoulders listening to the wireless looking for someone to gab to. It didn’t matter who, or what the conversation was about, he just liked gabbing, liked finding out what was going on in that person’s life, you might say.”

“A nosey type?”

"Yes, you're right there, a very nosy type and gossipy too! Anyway, it was on that same Friday evening, when Michael O'Connor happened to be strolling along the back alley on his way home from work, that he heard some loud banging noises coming from our back yard. Being the nosy type that he was, he does no more than pop his head around door and asks George what's going on."

"Hello George," he said, "you look busy. What're you up to son?"

"Just getting the last of these crates stacked," George told him, "before I go in for my tea."

"And what are they for?" Michael asked, pretending he didn't already know. "What are you planning to do with all these wooden crates?"

"I'm starting up a firewood business."

"A fire wood business?"

"Yes"

"In the backyard?" Michael said, raising his voice, "you can't do that." "Why not, what's wrong with that?"

"You could get yourself into serious trouble with the council doing things like that George, someone might report you."

"You're not thinking of reporting me are you Mike, because if you are..?"

"No, no, of course I'm not George," Michael interrupted, "but don't you agree it could be a little risky?"

"I'll have to take that chance? At least until I find somewhere else. There won't be enough room in this backyard anyway, not once the business starts growing the way I expect it will."

"I know of a place you can use George," Michael said, "and it won't cost you a penny in rent."

"Oh, where might that be?"

"It's very close to here. It's just up the road as a matter of fact, at the top end of Beaumont Street. It's an old stable at the back of the Pavilion Theatre belongs to my brother-in-law, he doesn't use it anymore."

"I don't understand how come it's rent free?"

"Because I'll pay the rent out of my own pocket George, that's why."

"You'll pay the rent? What are you talking about, why would you want to do that?"

"Partners George," Michael said, lowering his voice, looking around as if to check if anyone was listening. "I'll pay the rent if you'll let me become a partner. A kind of sleeping partner if you know what I mean. I think you might be on to a good thing here, in fact, I don't think you'll be able to cope on your own."

“Partners, who mentioned anything about partners? I’m not interested Mike, forget it.”

“Why not George, there’ll be plenty in it for both of us, especially with the two of us working at it. I mean, think about it George, this idea of yours could lead to much better things in the future.”

“Much better things, what are you talking about now?”

“Like a shop for instance.”

“A shop?”

“Yes, a shop, even two or three shops, what’s wrong with that? You’ve got to look ahead George, especially a young fella like you.”

“I’m going in,” your Dad told him, shaking his head. “I’ve finished now and I’m hungry.”

“If you ever want a hand chopping the crates George,” Michael shouted, “all you have to do is knock on our door. I’ve got a spare axe at home.”

“I’ve just told you, I don’t need a partner.”

“That’s fair enough George,” Michael said, “but I’d still like to help.”

“No thanks Michael, I’m really not looking for a partner. And with that he went inside the house to look for something for his dinner.”

“What did Grandad say when he saw all the crates in the backyard?”

“It was around ten thirty that evening when your Grandad arrived home from the pub, unaware that your Grandma and your Uncle Bill were sitting in the kitchen waiting for him. They rushed over to the window when they heard the back-door latch being raised, curious to know if he was sober enough to notice the pile of wooden crates stacked against the privy wall.”

“What the hell’s going on,” they heard him shout. “Where the bloody hell did all these things come from?”

“I’ll bet he was in a temper?”

“He certainly was. He was beside himself. I could even hear him shouting from my bedroom, the same bedroom you and Frank are in now.”

“What happened then?”

“I got up out of bed and stood on the landing so I could hear what was going on. That’s when I heard Bill open the scullery door to let your Grandad in.”

“Somebody’s got some bloody explaining to do,” your Grandad shouted as he pushed past Bill, “and they better be quick about it.”

“George wants to start up a little business of his own” Bill told your Grandad.

> "He doesn't need any interference from you. AND, I don't want you scrounging beer money from him. He's told me his plan is to try to make enough so Mother can give up scrubbing people's floors for a living!"

Grudgingly, your Grandad said

> "I'll give him a month to find somewhere else to run his firewood business from. Otherwise I'll report him to the council and they can come and throw all that mess out of MY yard. That's all I have to say on the matter!"

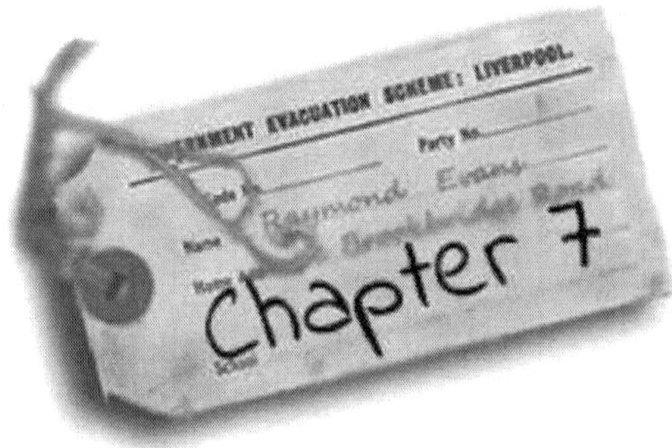

Firewood For Sale

The pram wheels were beginning to buckle under the weight as me and your Dad loaded the last few bundles of firewood.

"I don't care, just as long as it makes it to the street - otherwise we're in big trouble." Your Dad said

As luck would have it, we did make it into the street, but only just. Two of the wheels collapsed tipping most of the firewood out of the pram into the middle of the street. We looked at each other, shrugged our shoulders and started shouting on top of our voices as soon as we turned the corner into Cam Street:

"FIREWOOD FOR SALE!
TUPPENCE A BUNDLE!"

Almost immediately Mrs. Higgins' was out on the front step waving her purse in the air.

“I’ll have four bundles George,” she shouted, “I’ve got your money son, got it right here in my hand - eight pence, right?”

“Yes, that right Mrs. Higgins” George said.

“And next door wants some as well, George” she shouted.

“Thanks Mrs. Higgins” I said, “I’ll give her a knock”

“Everyone in the street knows about your firewood business George” Mrs. Higgins told him.

“I’ve been going round all day telling them about it.”

George was right; I think everyone in the street came out that day to buy firewood from us. Young George Evans was on his way - or so we all thought.”

“What do you mean by that, or so we all thought?”

“You’ll find out a little later when I get to the end of this story; we’re nearly there now.”

“Ok, but what happened when he got back to the house with all that money in his pocket. Was Grandad there, did he see the money?”

“Good question. No, your Grandad was not there. It was much too early for him to be home from the pub.”

“Can you remember how much money Dad had collected that night?”

"Can't remember exactly, somewhere around ten shillings I think."

"Was he pleased?"

"Oh yes. He was very pleased. Ten shillings was a lot of money in those days. I can still remember the delight on his face as he sat counting it all on the kitchen table. Your Grandma was so proud of him that night. We all were."

"What happened after that? You still haven't told me what you meant by 'or so we all thought'?"

"There you go again Ray, give me a chance son. I'm getting to that part of the story."

"Sorry Uncle Harold, it's just that I can't wait to find out what happened. I'm worried something bad happened."

"Well, things were going along quite nicely for your Dad. The business was growing stronger and stronger by the day. In fact it wasn't long before he was seriously thinking about giving in his notice. Maybe in a few weeks even, when he was hoping to have enough money to afford a sizeable deposit on the Donkey and Cart Michael O'Connor had told him about, the one Michael's brother-in-law wanted to sell."

"As it turned out, he wasn't able to, because shortly after that; things took a turn for the worse for your poor Dad."

"How?"

"Do you remember me talking about Thelma Hawkins at the beginning of this story?"

"Yes, she was the boss's daughter right?"

"That's right. Well it was her that found out about your Dad using the milk-float to carry the wooden crates - the one and only time he wasn't able to hire a handcart because they were all out on hire. She went straight to her father and told him about it, saying George should be sacked on the spot."

"How did she find out?"

"I don't know. We never did find out. But that wasn't all, what made matters worse, two people from the council turned up at the house that very same afternoon."

"What did they want?"

"Some busybody had gone and told them about your Dad using the back-yard to run his firewood business from."

"Was it Grandad? I'll bet that's who it was."

"Nope, you're wrong there, it wasn't your Grandad."

"Who was it then?"

"We were never able to prove it, but we all knew it was Michael O'Connor. Your Grandad went crazy. No sooner had the council men left the house; he was up stairs searching your Dad's things."

"Looking for Dad's money?"

"Yes."

"How much was there?"

"I don't remember how much."

"What did he do with it - spend it all in the pub?"

"Yes."

"All of Dads money?"

"Yes, every last penny went on him and all his drunken cronies. Your Dad finished up without his money and his job!"

"What about Michael O'Connor, what happened to him?"

"Michael O'Connor finally got his way by starting up on his own. In other words, he stole your Dad's firewood business without even offering him one miserly penny towards it."

It brought a lump to my throat listening to Uncle Harold tell me that story. Especially when he told how my father after all his hard work, lost everything through the greediness of my Grandfather and the trickery and deceit of Michael O'Connor.

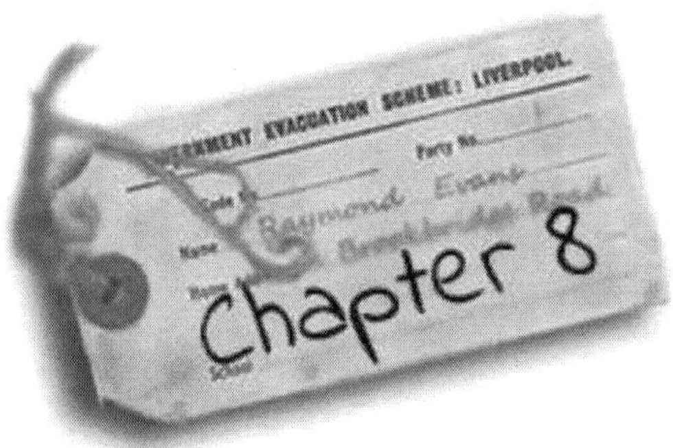

Hard Times & A Half Crown

Uncle Harold told me lots of stories about his early childhood days in Cam Street, when he and his brothers were young and going to school. I was consumed with an unending curiosity to learn as much as I could about my father as a young boy. For reasons best known to him, Uncle Harold would always refuse to speak about that particular period in his life, especially about my Grandfather. There weren't any photos to look back on other than a crinkled foggy black and white that stood all alone in the middle of the sideboard next to the clock. I always liked looking at that photo, seeing Grandma's pretty young face looking back at me.

Uncle Harold went on to tell me about the dreadful conditions he, his brothers and my Grandmother had to endure because of Grandad's heavy drinking. About the bullying and the beatings that took place when he came home drunk from the pub. How it broke his heart watching his mother sitting alone in the kitchen night after night darning socks and mending clothes while her husband was in the pub drinking her hard earned money away, causing the family to live constantly on the edge of poverty.

How his mother had to raise six boys on her own, while her grouchy cantankerous lazy good-for-nothing husband spent most of his life guzzling beer. In later years these same stories my Uncle told me helped me understand why my father held so much hatred towards my Grandfather.

A Half Crown coin equivalent to two shillings and six pence.
(Image UK Govt.wiki commons public domain)

The last time I saw my Grandfather was in the early part of 1954, just a few months before he died. I was leaving the house on my way to the bus stop when I hesitated at the front door. I caught sight of him walking down the street, stopping every few yards to lean on his walking-stick and catch his breath. What a sorrowful sight it was; a wizened lonely old man whose wife had passed on some years earlier.

"What are you looking at?" my mother asked, "I thought you were rushing to catch your bus"

"It's that man; I think it's Grandad" I said, "Why would he be coming here?"

"Oh, he's here every Tuesday" she said, "comes for his half-a-crown," (Two shillings and sixpence)

"Half-a-crown?"

"Yes, just like your Grandma used to. Don't you remember?"

"I do, but I thought Dad said he stopped it when Grandma passed away."

"He did, but I've carried on giving it to him."

"Does he still drink a lot?"

"Yes, when he can afford it. That's the reason your Dad doesn't like me giving him money, because he knows he'll spend it on beer instead of on food."

"He'll never forgive Grandad, will he?"

“No he won’t, especially for the way he treated your Grandma. He’ll never forgive him for that, I’m sure. Your Grandad was a bad man in those days, a man with a heart of stone.”

“I wonder if it plays on his conscience, now that Grandma’s gone and he’s all on his own?”

“I’m sure it does - every day of his life. That’s what happens to people like that,” Mum said, as she turned to go back for his money.

VE Day Victory

Dateline: May 7th, 1945 - Germany Surrenders.

At precisely 2:41AM, in a school building somewhere in Northern France, the unconditional surrender of all German, land, sea and air forces was finally signed. The German Foreign Minister later that day broadcast to his countrymen, telling them the war was now over.

At 7:40 PM on that same day the BBC interrupted a piano recital to announce that the following day (8th of May 1945) would be designated as Victory in Europe Day - V.E. DAY, and would be regarded as a holiday.

What a day that was. I can still remember looking down through the bedroom window watching the people opposite coming out of their houses into the street, openly kissing and hugging each other, shouting on top of their voices "It's all over!" – "Thank God it's all over!"

It was amazing. People came out of their places of work in snake-like processions dancing the Conga. The Church bells were rung for the first time since the start of the war. Ships horns were blown. They came out into the streets singing Vera Lynn's war songs, the same songs she sang to the troops throughout the five and a half years of the war. There'll Be Blue Birds over the White Cliffs Of Dover.' 'When They Sound The Last All Clear.' 'We'll Meet Again.'

As the evening closed in, the skies above the city began glowing brightly from the glare of giant bonfires people were lighting everywhere. Thousands of fireworks were set off. I have no idea where they got them from but I do remember thinking what an incredible sight it was.

It was hard to imagine that after six long years, the war had finally come to an end. Hard to imagine, there would be no more bombings, ever again. No more long cold damp nights sitting around in air raid shelters. No more blackouts. No more sinister whaling of sirens - a sound that never failed to send a wave of fear throughout your body which still makes my hair stand on end even to this day.

Mr. Shipman, a painter and decorator who lived down the street took a day off and used his longest ladder to help decorate Beaumont Street with Union Jacks and streamers. The local church loaned out trestle tables and chairs for the street party that our mothers were hastily arranging for the children. And not to be out done, factories, pubs, and shop keepers decorated their doors and windows with red, white and blue bunting and rosettes.

VE Day Street Party with a typical 'street' air-raid shelter in the background.(image source unknown)

The police gave permission for the people of Beaumont Street to build their bonfire on the bombsite directly across from Aunt Lucy's house, the same land where four houses once stood, tall gracious Victorian structures that had given a classic and distinctive charm to the neighborhood. They'd been razed to the ground by the Luftwaffe during the week of the 'May Blitz'.

Adolph Hitler didn't care where his pilots dropped their bombs; whether carelessly or deliberately. They dropped their screaming instruments of terror on hospitals,churches, schools, old people's homes, even on graveyards. Hitler wanted the stubborn British people to surrender and didn't care how his pilots went about ensuring that they did. It didn't matter to him how many innocent lives it would take, this mad man would do anything to accomplish his mission.

By this time Adolph Hitler was well known by everyone to be a person who lacked self-control. Someone who was very argumentative and bad tempered. He rejected offhand and with great hostility any advice or criticism that was offered. He was known to have a deep seated hatred and distrust of the Jewish people. During the war years, he had planned and overseen a vicious reign of genocide and cruelty upon the Jewish people and their communities throughout mainland Europe. The results of which were so horrific it's recorded in the annals of history as The Holocaust.

Hitler's long awaited demise had been splashed over every newspaper throughout the land, telling people how he had cowardly taken his own life deep down in his Berlin bunker on that last day of April, 1945, rather than face prosecution for his crimes.

"ADOLPH HITLER IS DEAD"

"ADOLPH HITLER COMMITS SUICIDE"

Many people who read those headlines wished Adolph had taken his life a little sooner, like six years sooner. Then perhaps over fifty million people would not have lost their lives in a nonsensical war that in the end would prove nothing and accomplish even less.

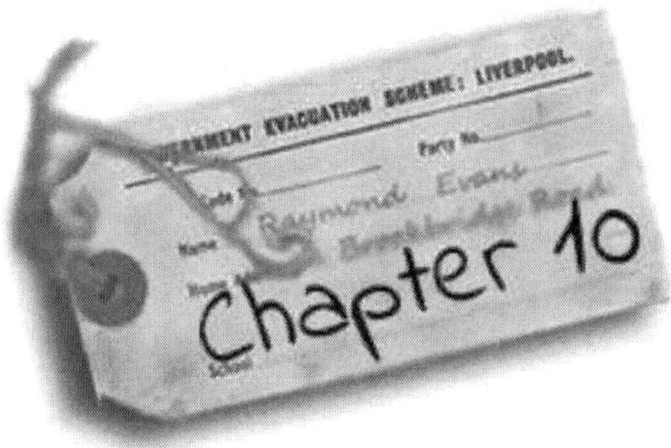

Canes Don’t Make Boys Able

Dateline: 14th May, 1945.

Nothing we had read in the papers or seen on the cinema screens could have prepared us for the horror and destruction we saw on the short journey to our new school that day.

The Luftwaffe’s incessant bombing raids left Liverpool a shabby, drab and battered city. It would take a long, long time to pull itself out of the ashes. Whole streets had been obliterated leaving acres of barren rubble strewn land where homes, shops, and churches once stood. Everywhere was a scene of utter devastation. I remember stopping to watch a group of clearance workers pulling down the remains of a bombed-out house (probably making room for another pre-fab to be built), thinking how very fortunate we were that our parents had made that important decision for us to evacuate. It was something that had never crossed my mind before, not until that very moment when I overheard one of the demolition workers telling one of his workmates, that there were seven people inside that home when it was struck by the bomb, three of them very young children.

I was six when we evacuated, and because we were a large family we could not be housed in the one place. So for six years I had been shunted among a total of six "foster homes". In the early years, I had some rough experiences and because I was so young, could not comprehend the circumstances nor understand the danger beyond how it impacted me. At one point, I had, very wrongly, come to believe that my Mother's motivation for allowing me to be separated from her and the family was to make life a little easier on her. In fact, nothing could have been farther from the truth.

*****

On arrival at the school we were directed to the headmaster's office for a quick-fire test to determine which grade or class we were to be assigned to. Class 'A' was for the clever ones, 'B' for the not so clever and 'C' for the dunces; the really 'thick' ones.

He was sitting at his desk silently evaluating and scribbling notes on some papers, stopping every now and then to dip his pen in the inkwell. Occasionally he would peer over the wire framed glasses precariously perched on the end of his nose to look us up and down. It wasn't until he'd finished writing that I got a proper look at his face; when I saw he had a glass eye, the one on the left. My younger brother Stan nudged me with his elbow.

“You’re being spoken to” he whispered.

“You weren’t listening, were you,” the headmaster said, sharply

“I just asked you a question.”

“Sorry sir, I didn’t know you were speaking to me.”

“You didn’t know because your mind was somewhere else. You were daydreaming instead of listening to what I was saying. I’ll ask you once more, and you had better get it right, otherwise you’ll feel this cane across your backside!”

“Yes sir!”

“Billy buys nine bars of chocolate costing 6d each, very quickly now, how much did Billy spend?”

“Four shillings and sixpence, sir!”

“Eighteen bars! How much did he spend for eighteen bars? QUICKLY –QUICKLYYY…”

“Nine shillings sir!”

“What’s the capital of Scotland?”

“Erm, Edinburgh?”

“Erm is not an answer! Are you asking or telling me?”

"Telling you sir, it is Edinburgh. I just couldn't think for a moment sir"

Fortunately, arithmetic was always a favourite subject of mine, and so was composition, but Geography I was never very good with. However, lucky for me on this day, I managed to scrape by.Looking back, the grungy old Granby Street school, (built I'm sure, just a year after Methuselah was born) could have easily claimed the highest illiteracy rate in the whole of Liverpool at the time.

The kids in that school were a wild lot to say the least - fights galore every single day. And not just in the playground, but quite often in the classroom whenever the teacher was out. The fact that there were fifty and sometimes sixty kids to a classroom was probably why the teachers had a hard time trying to keep control. Everything we'd been told about Granby Street School was turning out to be true. My two brothers and I hated every minute, and did so right up until the day we left, when we moved into a new house a year later.

The headmaster (a tall thin gangly man) for some strange reason always kept his cane hidden down the back of his jacket and would spend a large portion of his time peeking through the glass partitions looking for misbehavers. I can still remember quite clearly the first time he barged into our classroom screaming at the top of his voice...

"THAT BOY THERE, YOU IN THE CORNER, COME OUT HERE AT ONCE!"

I stood up on wobbly legs thinking he meant me.

"Me sir?" I said, in a low trembling voice, "but I wasn't..."

"NO, NO," he bawled

"NOT YOU... HIM SITTING NEXT TO YOU!"

"Do you mean me sir?" the boy asked, trying his best to look innocent.

"YES. YOU. YOU WITH THE GINGER HAIR, COME DOWN HERE, NOW!"

"Be forewarned every single one of you," the headmaster shouted, as he struck the air with a few practice swings. This is what will happen if you are caught talking or misbehaving in class. You'll get the same as he's about to get, either across your hands or across your backside; it's all the same to me!"

In case any of you young people reading this book, think I'm making this up I can assure you I'm not. That's what went on in those days. It wouldn't do any good to go home complaining to your parents either - even though your fingers and thumbs were swollen up to the size of a Cumberland sausage. The first thing parent's would say was "What were you doing? You must have been doing something wrong. You don't get caned for nothing."

So you can imagine how very frightened everybody was of this man in that place they called a school. If for instance, you ever felt the urge to talk in class, and everyone does at some time or another (I know I did), then the only possible way this could be achieved was to learn the technique of speaking like a ventriloquist, without moving your lips. That's what Ginger

Thompson; the boy who sat next to me suggested I should do. I took his advice and began practicing right away. There was no way that crazy headmaster is going to cane me, I told him, not if I can help it. So I practiced mostly at home in front of the bathroom mirror and sometimes in front of my brother Stan as he sat on the side of the bed.

I must admit though, I still feel a little guilty about what happened that day. After all it was my fault little Ginger Thompson got that terrible thrashing. If it hadn't been for me bothering him with questions every few minutes, preventing him from concentrating on his work, he wouldn't have lost his temper like he did. The headmaster wouldn't have caught him whispering in my ear telling me to shut up and 'go away' - or words to that effect.

Anyway, that's the way it was in those days. Break the rules and you got three stinging whacks typically with a half inch thick bamboo cane on each of your hands.

I didn't care much for school anyway. As a matter of fact, my attention (if I wasn't interested in a particular lesson, like say music for instance, which I found very boring) was always on the classroom clock. Miss Vickers, our music teacher, was one of those people who seemed to be overly impressed with herself. The kind of person who walked through life always looking down her long thin nose at people, the type you would enjoy pushing into a deep lake.

However, the lessons that did interest me the most, those I continued to get top marks for, were arithmetic, (always my favorite) followed by English, composition, drawing (Art), PT (physical training) and swimming.

Miss Critchely who taught arithmetic was without doubt my most favorite teacher of all. The only time I did stop liking her (which lasted for only a brief moment because of the strong boyhood crush I had on her) was the time she told me off for blurting out the answer to the long division sum she was halfway through writing on the blackboard. "That's the second time you've done that, Raymond Evans," she shouted, "now I'm going to have to start all over again because everyone knows the answer." Not sure where it came from, but I've always been rather quick with figures - the written ones, that is.

I couldn't wait to leave school, couldn't wait to get a job and bring home a wage packet like my older siblings were doing. From the age of six when I was first evacuated, and right up until I was about nine and a half (when they moved me and thirty other evacuees out of our temporary school into a proper school) we were never given a scrap of homework to do, or even a book to read for that matter. It wasn't the teachers fault; there was a war on. There was a drastic shortage of practically everything that was needed in a classroom. The teachers had to make do with what they were given.

Most of the people who were kind enough to take us into their homes were not really interested in our education; they weren't expected to be. They were in no way obligated to buy us books, help or give us homework. Their daily focus was pretty much on surviving day to day.

Education was something only rich people could afford to be concerned about. The working class just muddled through.

Times were difficult. The three R's – Reading, Writing and Arithmetic was really all you needed to learn.

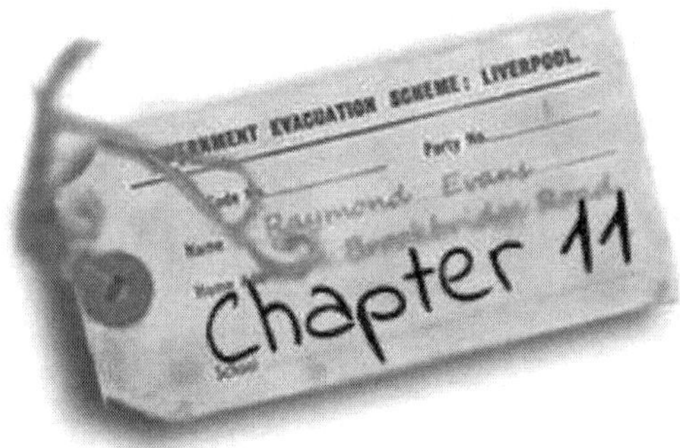

Big Bad Boly

I was assigned to Mr. Boldsworth's class; a big over weight Sherman Tank of a man, who, I'd been told had done a bit of professional wrestling in his time. The kids nicknamed him "Big Bad Boly" because he was always whacking one of us with his short fat bamboo cane.

It's only my second day in Big Bad Boly's class and I'm in trouble already. He's halfway through calling the register when he looks up and sees me fidgeting with something inside my desk. He slams the register down and races across the classroom like a mad Elephant.

> "What do you think you're doing Evans?" He says, pointing his cane at my face, "You're supposed to be sitting up straight with your arms folded looking directly at me, not gawping at something inside your desk, now put your hands on your head and don't take them down until I tell you to."

“Sorry sir, but the lid wouldn’t go down properly”

“The lid wouldn’t go down? Don’t be a bone head Evans; you really don’t expect me to believe that, do you?”

“No sir.”

“You’re a bone head, Evans, that’s what you are. We don’t like boneheads here, do we class?”

“NO SIR!”

“If there’s one thing I can’t abide, it’s a liar - d’you hear me Evans?”

“Yes sir!”

“And while we’re at it Evans, there’s one other little pet hate of mine I think you should know about.”

“Yes sir?”

“Absenteeism, people taking days off for no good reason like him sitting next to you. He’s always taking days off. Isn’t that right Clarkson?”

“Yes sir.”

“Take heed Evans, if you are ever absent, it better be because you’ve been run over by a bus on your way to school and you’ve died from your injuries.”

“Yes sir.”

Poor Alex Clarkson had sauntered into the classroom that morning twenty minutes late. He tried sneaking past the teacher while his back was turned writing on the blackboard. The teacher in his temper throws the chalk at the black-board and sprints after him.

"Where do you think you're going Clarkson?

"What's your excuse this time? Why are you late? Just got out of bed have you?"

"Erm..."

"Never mind erm! I've had enough of your excuses. In fact, I don't know why you even bother coming to school Clarkson? It may be a good idea for you ask your mother to put you in another school, a school that's far, far away from Granby Street School."

Alex says he's sorry and continues to make his way across the classroom towards his desk. Mr. Boldsworth grabs him by his collar and pulls him back. He wags his finger in his face and tells him not to walk away when he's being spoken to. Alex tries to apologize but the teacher shouts over him saying he's the laziest, scruffiest, can't get up in the morning type of child he's ever known in the whole of his life.

"You're too lazy to even comb your hair, you lazy little so and so. Look at yourself, your tie is all cock-eyed; your hair's all over the place and your shirt's buttoned up the wrong way."

Alex tries his best to explain his alarm clock is broken.

"What about your mother, can't she get you up?"

"Mum goes out to work early" Alex says, "She leaves at six o'clock. There's no one else to get me up."

"What about your father?"

"Don't have a Dad sir; he's dead."

Mr. Boldsworth is unfazed by any excuse poor little Alex tries to come up with. He clenches his teeth and wags his finger in Alex's face again giving him a stiff warning that if he's late once more he'll have the headmaster expel him from Granby Street School for ever.

That was the last time I saw Alex Clarkson, I've no idea what became of him, but at that moment I felt so sorry for him. It turned out he'd been an evacuee just like me and this was what he'd come "home" to. It was apparent for whatever reason, he'd earned the intense hatred of this teacher, and even worse, Boldsworth was in a position of authority where he could make this poor lad's life an absolute misery.

Granby Street was a terrible school. My brothers and I hated it more and more each day. On any given day, I'd have gladly volunteered to suffer a visit to the dentist and have a tooth extracted than go to that school. There was always bullying of some sort going on every single day. Mostly at playtime or at the end of the day when school let out. Usually the trouble was instigated by a certain gang of thugs roaming around the schoolyard looking for trouble.

Their leader, 'Big Sammy Prescott' was a thug, a bully and a thief. He would inexplicably take a dislike to someone and then visit an endless barrage of hostility on them. Typically they would be much younger and smaller than him. Even some of the teachers were frightened of big Sammy Prescott. Because of his size, the big fat roly-poly lump of lard could wield more power in the schoolyard than Field Marshal Montgomery was able to do in the wide open Desert. There were lots of reasons why Sammy liked being the leader of a gang. His favourite was wielding the power to choose which person he thought deserved a good bashing up that day.

My brother Albert was unfortunate enough to find himself Sammy's target just the other day. Sammy started the trouble by knocking Albert's glasses to the floor and stomping on them. Now our Dad had always taught us that bullying needs to be dealt with "head-on", otherwise life would be unbearable. They will continue to pursue and persecute you until life becomes unbearable, he would tell us. So it's better to nip it in the bud right at the start.

Dad had always said coming home from school complaining about bullies wouldn't solve anything. You just have to get in first, hit them as hard as you can, right – flat – on the nose. If you do that, he won't come back looking for more - bullies never do. They're counting on their reputation as a bully to make most people back off or run away. You need to stand up to them. Fight fast and hard. Deck him before he knows what's coming!

Albert, (normally quiet and mild mannered) in his temper lunged at Sammy and hit him flat on his nose, just like Dad had taught him. Sammy, blood spurting from his nose, fell backwards onto the concrete floor dazed and confused. Albert then calmly stepped back, took position in-between Stan and me, waved his fists at Sam's gang of thugs and began handing them a stiff warning to keep their distance, otherwise they'd get their heads smashed in by ALL three of us. Stan turned to Albert and in a low voice, said to him,

"All three of us? Are you MAD?"

Fortunately, Albert's words of warning were lost in the shriek of Mr. Hill's whistle who quickly marshaled us back to our classrooms.

*****

Directly opposite the school gates stood Stoneham's Bakery Shop and Café. A flourishing business that was first started somewhere around the nineteen twenties. Stoneham's was the only shop in that scruffy seedy area that I had no qualms in spending the last penny of my pocket money. People came from all over for their legendary meat pies and custard tarts, often queuing outside long before the shop was open. I remember finding a sixpence [6d] outside of a pub one morning on my way to school. I couldn't wait for lunch time to come around so I could splurge it on three hot, fresh juicy pork pies, one each for Albert, Stan and me.

Just like many of the other shops in that area, Stoneham's windows were broken on so many occasions by Sammy Prescott and his Granby Street thugs, the bakery was eventually forced to close down and move to another safer location a few miles away. That was a crying shame in my book, because it meant no more crusty cobs to go with the bottle of free milk we were given during our morning break

Dad Is De-Mobbed

Dateline: June, 1945.

It was around this time (I can't remember the actual date) that my father and my eldest brother George were de-mobilized; Dad from the Royal Air Force, and George (a couple of weeks later) from the Welsh Guards.

Dad, now in his 44th year had spent the previous three and a half years treating the wounded and sick in a military hospital out in the Middle East in a place called Aden. During his time with the Royal Air Force they had trained him as a male nurse, a profession he immediately fell in love with and which subsequently influenced the rest of his life.

Wanting to further his knowledge of the medical profession, he was eager to take advantage of the special provisions the government was offering to ex-servicemen and attend medical classes at 'Broadgreen Hospital', where he later found work.

The fact that Dad was by far the oldest pupil in his class and the least educated; did not deter him in any way. He joined the local library and spent all his spare time reading medical books. He even took them to bed with him, keeping Mum awake into the early hours of the morning so she could quiz him. Dad wasn't satisfied with being a nurse anymore; he wanted to be a State Registered Nurse. He wanted his S.R.N certificate, and "nothing on God's green earth", he told my mother, was going to stop him from achieving that goal. His dedication and hard work finally paid off enabling him to pass his exams at the very first attempt. He was now a fully-fledged State Registered Nurse, quite an achievement (especially for someone who left school with very little education) and feat we all admired him greatly for.

My brother George on the other hand, put on his dark blue, pin-striped de-mob suit and trilby and tried his hand at being a brush and vacuum cleaner salesman. I think he stuck it out for maybe a couple of months before deciding to move on to better things. He got himself a far better paying job working for a large chemical company located in the small town of Northwich.

Dateline: 8th April,1946.

The man in the council office shuffled his papers:

"I'm sorry Mrs. Evans," he said, as he handed my mother the keys, "It's the best we can offer you at the moment."

"But I thought you were moving us into one of the new houses in Gillmoss. We've been waiting for over a year now."

"Sorry Mrs. Evans. There's nothing else we can do right now"

"Where is this house exactly?"

"Halfway down Jubilee Drive Mrs. Evans, opposite Kensington Park gates. The directions are all there on the paper I've just handed you."

"How bad of a state is the house in? According to your letter it'll need a good cleaning before we can even move in."

"Pretty bad, I'm afraid. And yes, it does need a good cleaning."

"What kind of people lived there, leaving it in that state?"

"Army personnel; officers and the like; they moved out about a year ago, not long after the war ended. It's been empty ever since."

"Army Officers?"

"Yes. The house was taken over by the government at the beginning of the war."

"How long do you think we'll have to wait for one of the new houses they're building in Gillmoss?"

"A year, maybe longer, I'm not sure. There are thousands of people waiting for houses, Mrs. Evans, the list is endless. You have to understand; it's an impossible task for the council. You may not be aware of it, but there are still quite a few families living in bomb damaged buildings, places that don't have electricity, gas, or even running water."

Dateline: 25th April, 1946.

Jubilee Drive stretches about a half mile from Kensington through to Edge Lane. Brick terraced houses on one side and a park on the other. Every house looks exactly the same, tall Victorian houses with rusty spiked railings along the front. A high brick wall borders the flagstone yard at the rear and is topped with countless pieces of broken green and brown beer bottles set in cement.

The brick built 'privy' in the backyard stinks to high heaven in the summer and freezes solid in the winter. A heavily bolted door leads to the back alley, a narrow lane that runs behind the houses where mangy cats live and everybody's smelly bins are kept. The house inside is much larger than it looks from the outside. It's got four good sized bedrooms, a bathroom and toilet, a parlor, a dining room, a kitchen, a scullery and last but not least, a dark dank basement where the gas meter and the coal is kept. The coalman comes around once a week to deliver the coal one sack at a time by way of the coal hole located at the bottom of the front steps.

"You four boys will be sleeping up here in the attic," my mother says, gesturing to the four narrow wooden beds lined up against the wall. "Two at this end in the alcove and two at the far end opposite the door. I'll leave it to you to decide who's sleeping where - I'm much too busy right now."

With that she hurries out of the bedroom to organize my sisters Elsie and Muriel as they help with the unpacking.

"Right," Frank says, in his sergeant major voice, "you two in the alcove, me and Albert at the far end - all agreed?"

Stan and I nod in agreement knowing full well it would be futile to do otherwise. As it was, I quite liked the idea of sleeping in the little alcove, and so did Stan for that matter. We liked the way the ceiling sloped down to finger touching height above our beds.

"It's like having our own little bedroom," Stan says, as we climb into our beds on that first night.

"Yes," I tell him, "I love this house, don't you?"

"Yeah," he says, "I'm glad the war is over and we're all back together again."

"Yeah, so am I. By the way, what happened to our house in Brookbridge Road. Did it really get bombed?"

"Yeah, it did, didn't you know?"

"No, I didn't. Remember I was separated from everybody when we were evacuated."

“Well it did. Mum and Dad lost practically everything. That’s why we had to go live in Aunt Lucy’s house when we got back from South Wales. Mum and Dad have had to start all over again.”

“So is that why we’re sleeping on camp beds instead of proper beds?”

“Yes, Dad bought them from the Army and Navy stores the other day.”

“They’re not very comfortable; they’re making my back ache already.”

“I know,” Stan said, “same here. Listen, we better get to sleep before Frank comes up, he doesn't like you talking in bed, not even whispering.”

With that, and despite how uncomfortable the camp beds were, and the fact that they made very loud creaking noises each time you made the slightest move, my brother Stan, (as always) fell asleep almost immediately. I on the other hand tossed and turned for a little while longer until I too drifted off into a deep sleep.

"Wake up, wake up," I faintly heard Frank saying.

Next thing I know, I'm sitting bolt upright in bed, my heart thumping against my ribs thinking we’ve been bombed and the house is on fire.

“What’s the matter, what’s wrong?” I sputtered, still half asleep.”

“You’re breathing too loud," he said, "keep it down, just-keep-it-down. I can't get to sleep."

“Breathing too loud? Are you serious? You mean you woke me just to tell me I’m BREATHING TOO loud?”

"Yes," he said, making his way back to his bed, "it’s very annoying!"

"Put your head under the bedclothes," Stan whispered, "that's what I always do. You won't have to do it for too long, he'll be asleep in a couple of minutes."

all I want is a peaceful world and a pork pie!

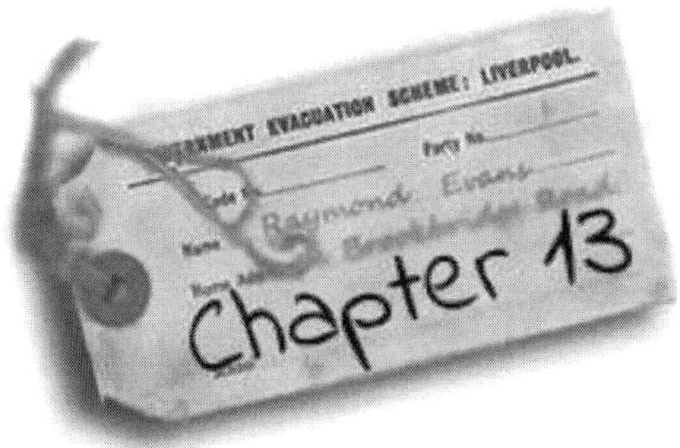

Uncle Dicky & A Dog

Dateline: 24th May, 1946.

Its Albert's birthday today, born in 1932 on 'Empire day'. That's how he got his name, mum naming him after Prince Albert (as if Albert gives a toss). And because he's turned fourteen, (the school leaving age) he'll soon be looking for a job, a skilled job that is, a trade.

Uncle Dicky, a man devoid of ambition. Who's had scores of jobs since he and the world of academics parted company at the tender age of fourteen, called at the house the other day to ask my mother if she was interested in buying a dog.....a dog?

"It's house trained," he told her,

"I did make sure of that before I parted with me money."

"A dog?" My mother said, looking somewhat puzzled.

"Yes, I bought it for the wife, for her birthday."

“The wife? Don’t you mean Julia?”

“Yes, Julia.”

“Then say Julia,” my mother said, “*The Wife* sounds awful.”

“Well anyway, she doesn’t want it, that’s me problem, Beatrice. That’s why I was hopin’ you’d take it from me, you know, for the kids, like.”

“You mean you want your money back? Is that what this is all this about?

“Well, yes.”

“Where did you buy this dog from - a pet shop?”

“Nope, got it from a fella I met in the pub; gave him two quid for it.”

“Two pounds? That’s a lot of money, Richard, especially if it’s a mongrel? It **is** a mongrel, right?”

“No, it’s not a mongrel it’s a cross-breed. That’s what he told me anyway. He said it’s got a bit of a Collie in it. Please take it from me, I need the money.”

“Then the dog **is** a mongrel, Richard - take it from me.”

“It is?”

“Yes. Oh and by the way, did you get that job you were telling me about, delivering coal?”

“Yes. I started last week, but I don’t get paid till tomorrow. So, what do you think? Will you take the dog?”

“Yes, alright, I’ll take him off your hands. What’s his name?”

“It’s a she, her name’s Peggy.”

“Where’s the dog now?”

“Outside tied up to the railings. Is Albert in?”

“Yes. Why?”

“There’s a job going if he’s interested.”

“Where?”

“Same place where I’m workin’.”

“Go and ask him while I get the dog, he’s upstairs in the attic with Stanley and Raymond playing darts.”

“There’s a job going in our place if you’re interested,” he says to Albert.

“What kind of job?” Albert asks, excitedly.

“Working with me delivering bags of coal to houses and shops, its heavy work but the money’s good, really good.”

“But that’s not a trade” Albert says, “Dad says I’ve got to have a trade.”

“Well, I just thought I’d mention it in case you were interested, that’s all” Uncle Dickey says, “I mean you are looking for a job aren’t you?”

“Yes I am Uncle Dicky, “Albert says, “in fact there’s a job here in the paper I wouldn’t mind applying for - training to be a butcher.”

“Is that what you fancy doing; becoming a butcher?”

“Well, yes, what’s wrong with that? It is a trade.”

“A trade it may be,” Uncle Dickey says “But what’s the good of that if you’re going to be paid peanuts?”

Well, I know it’ll be low pay at first, Dad’s already explained that to me.”

“Maybe so, but I don’t think your mum will like the money they’ll be paying you, won’t even be enough to feed you for a week, and that’s without paying out for clothes, shoes, bus fare and the like. Give it a couple of months, see how you go. Don’t forget, your Mum needs the money.

You’ll get a lot more at Ashford’s where I work, double in fact. And anyway, I’ve told my boss already, he’s very short handed at the moment, he’s looking for strong young lads like you. Young lads that have just left school and are looking for work, looking to earn lots of money. Mr. Ashford’s really looking forward to meeting you, Albert”

“And it’s definitely double what I’ll get in the butchers?”

“Yes, could even be more with overtime.”

“But I’m not sure if I can lift a bag of coal, Uncle Dicky. “Are the bags very heavy?”

“They all weigh the same, a hundredweight.”

“Wow that sounds really heavy? I’m not sure if I’ll be able to lift that much weight, Uncle Dickey?”

“Of course you will, once you get used to it. It’s a knack, that’s all. There’s nothing to it. Don’t worry about it Albert, I’ll show you.”

“What time would I have to start?”

“Eight o’clock. But if you get there a few minutes earlier, say about a quarter to eight, I’ll teach you how to harness up Daisy and back him into the shafts.”

“Did you say Daisy then Uncle Dickey?” I ask interrupting the conversation.

“Mind your own business and stop interrupting,” Albert says. “It’s nothing to do with you.”

“But Daisy is a Cow’s name. Why would Uncle Dickey’s boss name his horse Daisy?”

“It was me that gave him the name,” Uncle Dickey says, “not my boss. Now if you don’t mind Raymond, go back to your darts because I’d like to continue this conversation with your brother.”

"Sorry Uncle Dickey, but I don't understand why anyone would give a horse a name like Daisy, especially if it's a male horse?"

"Why? What the hell's wrong with the name Daisy?"

"Because I thought cows were called Daisy, that's why."

"Why don't you use your loaf Raymond," Uncle Dickey says, becoming more and more agitated, "and stop interrupting and asking silly questions? What difference does it make anyway what name I've given the bloody animal, it's a horse for God's sake, he doesn't know any different. I'm sure he won't be going around complaining to the other horses about his name."

After being told about Uncle Dickey talking Albert into becoming a coal man, my father that evening, felt a strong desire to slip his coat back on and pay Uncle Dicky a visit. Fortunately for Uncle Dicky, my mother managed to talk him out of it.

"I'm trying to set you up with a trade," he told Albert, "do you understand? I'm trying to ensure your future prosperity. Do not take any notice what your Uncle Dickey tells you - ever

"But Dad, I've already told him I'll take the job. I can't let him down now, not after him buying us a dog. And anyway Dad, the money's good. It's double what I'll get in the butchers."

"That's as maybe, but good money or not, you need a trade. Lugging heavy bags of coal around is not going to get you anywhere. And anyway, your Uncle Dickey won't last five minutes before he's on the move again. The longest job that man's ever held is milk monitor at school. He'll be off again looking for something else. He's always changing jobs.

"Can I at least try it then? Just to see what it's like."

"If that's what you want, then yes, go ahead. I don't mind, but you'll be looking for something better in a few weeks anyway, you mark my words"

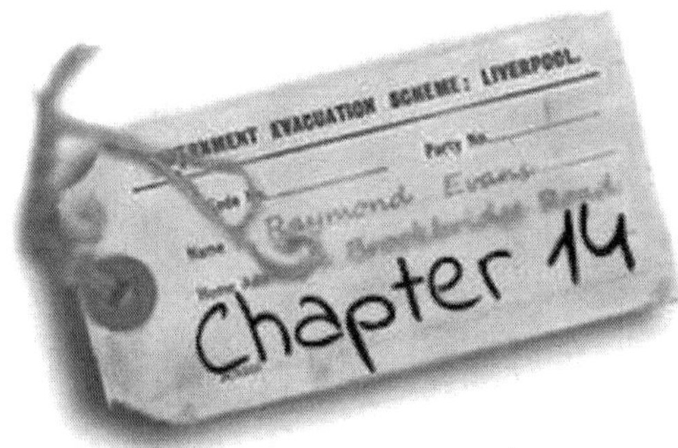

Coal In The Wrong Hole

Two weeks later:

My mother is busy ironing her way through the usual mountain of clothes when she hears the kitchen door opening. She turns around and sees Albert, black as the ace of spades, standing in the doorway with a worried look on his face.

"Good God Albert, you gave me the fright of my life. I didn't recognize you at first, where've you been son, up a chimney?

"Sorry Mum if I frightened you."

"It's early for you to be home isn't it? Did something happen?"

"I've been sacked mum."

"Sacked! What on earth for, son?"

"It was raining heavy, so my glasses misted up, I couldn't help it. I made a mistake that's all it was. Anyone can make a mistake."

"Raining heavy, mistake, what are you talking about, Albert?"

"I tipped three bags of coal down the wrong hole. It was a mistake."

"What do you mean son, down the wrong hole?"

"I emptied Mrs. Timpson's three bags of coal into the sewer by mistake."

"You didn't?" She felt for poor Albert as he was obviously distressed so she worked hard to stifle a laugh.

"Yes I did. The two manholes were right next to each other and I was rushing. I got them mixed up."

"Oh dear, what did Mr. Ashford say?"

"He's given me the sack and docked three shilling and sixpence from my wages."

"Three shillings and sixpence, what on earth for?"

"To pay for the three bags of coal I dumped down the sewer."

"Oh dear, well never mind son."

"He's sacked Uncle Dickey as well, mum."

"Uncle Dickey? Why?"

"For not watching what I was doing, for not supervising me properly."

"Never mind, don't get yourself all upset about it. I didn't like you working there anyway. Go jump in the bath, you'll feel much better after a good hot soak."

"Sorry Mum," Albert says; "I'll start looking for something else right away but something with a trade this time."

"What about that job in the State Restaurant your Dad was talking about the other day, training to become a chef? Now that's much better than carrying heavy bags of coal on your back, I'm sure."

*****

A few weeks later:

"What do you mean, you don't like the job?" Dad says. "You told me you liked the idea of becoming a chef."

"I do Dad, but I'm just a washer-upper," Albert says, "All I do is wash hundreds of greasy pots and pans all day long. I'm supposed to be training to become a chef, not a washer-upper."

"You have to start at the bottom of the ladder in any job. Good God, you've only been in the job five minutes, give it a couple of more weeks, at least."

"Two more weeks at being a washer–upper - they told

me in the interview it would only be for a few days. Nah, I don't fancy that Dad. That's worse than being a coal man."

"Go see your boss then. That Italian fella you're always talking about, Mr. Montinelli or whatever his name is. Go see him on Monday morning. Knock on his office door and tell him straight. Be firm. Tell him you came there to be a chef, not a washer-upper. See what he says. He can't sack you just for asking."

Albert gets his promotion working in the hors oeuvres kitchen under the strict supervision of Chef Jack Sutton. Now he can't stop talking about the place, saying how much he likes his new job. Mr. Martinelli is so pleased with him he's even given him a raise of two shillings a week.

"That's good," Dad tells him. "Now you're getting somewhere. But don't forget, a shilling of your rise has to go towards the housekeeping."

"I know Dad. I've already arranged that with Mum. But listen, this restaurant where I'm working, it's really posh inside. You should go and see it. It's the classiest restaurant in town, you can ask anyone."

"And the most expensive as well, I've no doubt," Dad says. "I've always wanted to take your Mother there but never been able to afford it.""I know, you can't even get a cup of tea for under sixpence," Albert says, "Imagine that, paying all that money out for just one lousy cup of tea?"

Earning My Keep

I'm on my way home from school one day, when my mate tells me about a newspaper job that's going."

"What's the name of the shop?"

"Story's Newsagents and Tobacconist," he says.

"How did you find out about it?"

"I know the lad that worked there," he says, "Arthur Mullins. He lives in our street. He's been given the sack."

"What for?"

"Stealing."

"Stealing, you're kiddin'?"

"No I'm not kidding. He couldn't keep his fingers out of the old lady's toffee jars, could he? She even caught him with his fingers in the cash-draw one day. He told her some story about her leaving the cash draw open and that he was just closing it for her. He's been told never to set foot in the shop ever again; or any of his family for that matter."

"Where's the shop – is it the one at the top end of Kensington?"

"It's just down the street from where you live, next door to the Chemist on the corner of Farnsworth Street."

The next day on my way home from school I check if the sign is still in the window like my mother suggested.

'Delivery boy wanted for morning newspaper route.
Must be honest, hard-working and punctual.
Apply Within.'

After a very short interview, Mrs. Story surprises me by asking if I can start tomorrow morning.

"Yes I can, Mrs. Story."

"Good," she says, "but you must be here at ten minutes to six so you can start your deliveries at six o'clock sharp, no later. Do you think you can manage that, Raymond?"

"Yes Mrs. Story. I can manage that easily, and I won't be late, I promise. I'm never late for anything.

"Are you sure now Raymond? Because it's very important you're here on time. You'll have to be up much earlier than when you're going to school."

"Oh yes, I'm very sure, Mrs. Story."

"I've never met you before Raymond, so I hope I'm correct in thinking you are a trustworthy person?"

"Yes, Mrs. Story, I am a very trustworthy person."

"Your wages will be four shillings a week, plus a bag of sweets every Saturday, but that's a bonus you only get for good time keeping."

"Thank you Mrs. Story, thank you very much."

I took pride in earning my own keep; couldn't wait to get started. I was allowed to keep a shilling out of my wages for pocket money; the rest was given over to my mother as my contribution towards the household expenses.

However, my first morning doesn't start too well. I'm at the third house and I've already got a problem. No matter how much I try, I can't get the letter box to open. I keep pushing hard but it just will not budge. It's jammed tight, almost as if it's been screwed down. I start to get a little panicky.

What am I supposed to do now? Should I ring the bell? No, it's too early; they might still be in bed. There's only one thing left to do, I'll have to come back later when they're up.

I'm making my way to the next house when an old lady leans out of her bedroom window and shouts down to me, wakening up the whole street. Swearing like a trouper she was, really bad words you would not expect from a woman of her age. The little dog she's got tucked under her arm keeps barking, making it difficult to hear what she's saying. It's one of those bad tempered little dogs, ankle-biters as my Dad calls them. Those that are never happy until they've got their needle sharp teeth sunk well into your leg.

> "Hey you," she shouts, "where do you think you're going with my bloody newspaper? Bring it back here, right now."
>
> "Sorry missus but the letter box wouldn't open..."
>
> "It's sealed; couldn't you see that, turnip head?"
>
> ***Turnip head?***
>
> "Sorry, I didn't know it'd been sealed."
>
> "You didn't know? What are you talking about? You've been coming here long enough?"
>
> "No missus, I haven't. I'm the new paper boy, this is my first day."
>
> "Then why didn't you ring the bell instead of trying to force the letter-box off its bloody hinges and upsetting my little Henry here?"

That's when it hits me, when I suddenly remember Mrs. Story warning me about this lady's letter box, telling me not to try forcing it because she'd had it sealed. It was the very last thing she told me before leaving the shop.

"She's a little strange, a little bit odd" she'd said as she handed me the large canvas bag full of newspapers. "So don't try fiddling around with the letter box, or you'll start the dog barking and that'll get her annoyed. She doesn't like things being put through her letter box, her dog chews them up. You must wait until you've finished your paper round before you deliver her newspaper, she'll be up and about by then. That's what the other newspaper boy used to do."

I was so concerned with getting done on time, or maybe even faster than the last boy did, that conversation with Mrs. Story had gone right out of my head until this moment.

"I'm sorry missus; I thought the letter box was jammed."

"You're supposed to ring the bell or knock on the door; didn't Mrs. Story tell you that? And anyway, where's the other lad that normally delivers the papers, what's wrong with him, still lazing in bed I wouldn't wonder?"

"I've just told you missus, he's left. I'm the new paper boy now."

"He's left, and Mrs. Story never told you about my letter box?"

"No, I lied, it must have slipped her mind - she forgot to tell me."

"Well, stay right there where you are and don't you move, I'll come down and get it."

"No, it's alright Missus, I'll bring it back later, there's no need for you to come down right now, go back to bed."

"NO! I don't want it bringing back later, and don't tell me what to do either, you cheeky little sod. Do as you're told and stay right where you are. I'll be down as soon as I've got my dressing gown and slippers on. Good God, you're as bad as that other bloody idiot."

"But what if your dog gets out missus?"

"Get out, get out? Don't be such a baby. Look at him? Look at the size of him, there's nothing of the little fella; he's frightened of his own bloody shadow for God's sake."

My Dad's words about small-ankle-biter-type dogs rang in my ears as I thought

That's what they all say!

I can hear a slow shuffle as she makes her way down the hallway toward the door. She opens it just wide enough for me to get a clear view of lean-mean-snapping machine Henry's needle sharp teeth.

"Stupid little bugger," she shouts, snatching the paper out of my hand, "now sod-off before I lose my temper."

Finally I was able to trudge on in the pelting rain, my feet squelching in my boots, the strap on the canvas bag digging ever deeper into my shoulder. I had six more streets to do, sixty something more houses.

> ***I'll never get this paper round finished - everything's going wrong. She'll sack me when I get back, I know she will, and it's only my first day.***

Three hours later, an hour longer than it should have taken to finish the round, I limped into the house like a drowned rat, my hair plastered to my head and my wet socks rolled up in a tiny ball under my feet.

> "It won't always be like that," my mother said, "It was your first day. See how things turn out tomorrow, then if you still don't like it, you'll just have to give Mrs. Story a week's notice, won't you? "

My mother was right; everything was so different the next day. Even the sun came out before I was halfway round the route. I woke at five that morning, half an hour before the alarm was due to go off. This allowed me sufficient time to make a cup of tea, and a couple of rounds of toast which I plastered with the usual thick layer of Tate & Lyles Golden Syrup. Then, not wanting to disturb anyone, I grabbed my cap and coat and left through the back door and along the back alley.

There was a full moon and the sky was filled with bright twinkling stars. It felt wonderful even though it was cold enough to make my teeth chatter. But I didn't care; it was as if I had the whole city to myself. I raced down the empty street eager to get started. Mrs. Story glanced down at her watch when I entered the shop.

> "You're early Raymond," she said, "I haven't even finished marking the papers yet."

“That’s okay Mrs. Story,” I said, “Just give me the ones you’ve already done, the ones for Leopold Road across the street. By the time I’ve finished delivering them, you’ll have finished marking up the rest.”

Newspaper Nightmares

About a month later:

It's a Saturday afternoon. I've just walked into the shop after finishing the paper round. Mrs. Story hands me my bag of sweets and asks if I'd be interested in delivering the Sunday papers as well as the daily papers.

"The boy that usually does the Sunday papers has been coming in late," she says, "I'm getting complaints every week from the customers."

"How much extra would I get paid, Mrs. Story?"

"Because it's Sundays, I'll pay you two shillings and sixpence for delivering the papers and sixpence for

collecting a few paper bills – three shillings altogether.

"Three shilling, that means my wages will go up to seven shillings a week then, is that right, Mrs. Story?"

"Yes, that's correct, but you'll be working seven days a week don't forget, not six."

"It doesn't matter. It doesn't bother me working seven days a week Mrs. Story. I can do it. I'd rather earn the extra money."

"The Sunday newspapers have supplements making them much heavier to carry," she says, "So I've decided to buy a delivery bike for you to carry them in. It's getting delivered tomorrow. One like the butcher uses to deliver his meat. Do you know the type I mean with a big metal basket on the front? You'll be able to put the newspaper bag inside that."

"Yes I do."

"You can ride a bike, I take it Raymond?"

"Yes Mrs. Story, I can. When do you want me to start delivering the Sunday papers?"

"Next Sunday."

"What time do want me here?"

"Eight o'clock, but you better ask your parents first. I want to be sure they agree in letting you work Sundays."

"They won't mind Mrs. Story; they'll leave it up to me."

"Ask them anyway, just to make sure. Ask them would they please give you a signed note agreeing to it."

*****

The Sunday newspapers are much thicker and heavier than the week-day papers, but I'm not bothered because I don't have to carry the bag over my shoulder any more, only the leather cash bag where I keep the money. It's got three pockets, one for pound notes, one for ten shilling notes and one for coins. I like collecting the newspaper money because it not only makes me feel important, but I make a lot of tips as well. Some are a little slow putting their hands in their pockets, while others are quite generous. For instance, as well as a glass of Sarsaparilla and a piece of home-made fruit cake, one old lady who I think (going by the size of her house and fancy looking furniture) is very rich, always slides a sixpence in my jacket pocket just as I'm leaving. A whole sixpence all for myself! She's my favorite customer, so far.

*****

One thing I had to learn very quickly was never to get the newspapers mixed up, which is exactly what I did a few days after I first started, when I delivered Mr. Samuel's, (a crusty old curmudgeon if ever there was one) 'Daily Mail' instead of the 'Daily Mirror'. He was so upset he came running after me in the middle of the street waving his arms in the air yelling at the top of his voice:

> “Hey you, you’ve given me the wrong paper. I’m supposed to get the Daily Mirror, not this bloody Daily Mail you’ve just stuffed through my letter box.”
>
> “Sorry Mr. Samuel, I must have got them mixed up.”
>
> “Sorry, I should bloody think you **are** sorry. This is a Capitalist paper you just stuffed through my letter box, that’s what this is. A newspaper owned by a lot of posh Tory bastards who couldn’t organize a piss-up in a brewery. Those that want to run the country for their own profit. I wouldn’t have it in the house if it were free, wouldn’t even use it for toilet paper.”

Then, suddenly before I’m able to stop him, he snatches the bag out of my hand and tips the newspapers out onto the wet pavement in search of his Daily Mirror. It was looking like he was about to have a heart attack the way he was carrying on, and all over a newspaper. He even made a special trip down to the shop later that day trying to get me the sack. He told Mrs. Story it wasn’t the first time it had happened, that it happened just a week ago when I mistakenly got his paper mixed up with next door’s paper. It seemed he was determined to get me sacked and all over one measly little mistake. Mrs. Story asked him to calm down and stop swearing. But he just kept going on and on about it, getting louder and louder, until she finally told him to get out of her shop and that she didn’t want his custom anymore. That he should go and buy his Daily Mirror somewhere else. I was really glad when she told me that. Now, whenever I see him in the street, I give him one of my secret two-finger 'V' signs, the one I do inside my coat pocket.

It didn't bother me getting up early each morning, not even in the winter when it was raining or snowing. Delivering newspapers taught me a lot about what was going on in the world. Whenever I was early getting around, I'd stop for a couple of minutes to have a quick read. Having even just a little money in my pocket made me feel important and independent.

> "Be careful how you spend it," Dad would say, "always save a little."

And that's exactly what I did, putting the odd few pennies in my Post Office Savings Bank account every week.

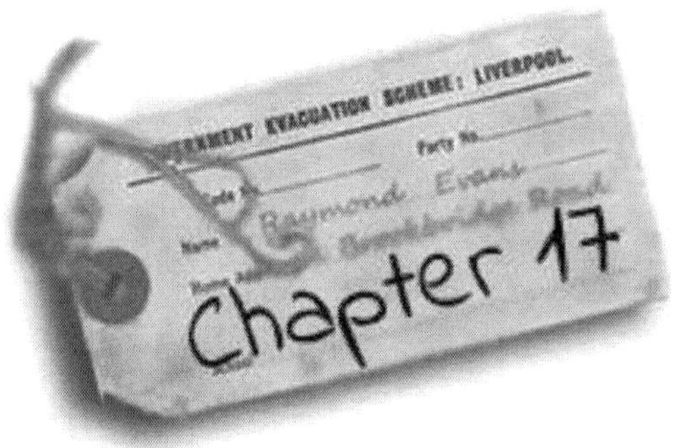

School's Out...Maybe

1947 had seen the worst winter in nearly a hundred years. Power cuts, coal rationing and scores of transport strikes, all brought the country to its knees. Those who'd voted for the Labour Government were now having second thoughts wishing Mr. Churchill was back in power.

Fortunately as bad as things were, even with the loss of George's contribution to the household (he'd moved out to Northwich to be closer to his work) it was having little effect on the Evans house-hold. Elsie, Franky, Muriel and Albert had all settled into good paying jobs enabling Mum to afford new things for the house. Topping her list was an electric fire and two fireside chairs for the parlor, followed by new carpets and lace curtains for the kitchen and dining room. She even managed a second-hand wind-up gramophone that she bought from Silverman's Pawnbroker's. Impatient to try it out, Frank went out that same day and bought two long playing records - 'Twelfth Street Rag' and 'My Yiddisher Mamma.' The trouble was, because he played those two records none-stop for what must have been close on a week, was the reason the old gramophone finally groaned to a stop, never to be played again.

One of the things I still do remember so vividly about 1947 was the day Mrs. Story told me about the school leaving age being raised. That put me in a right grumpy mood, especially after tramping around in knee deep snow delivering newspapers for two and a half hours. I went straight into the kitchen when I got home and told my mother:

> "Some bone-headed busybody government official has come up with the bright idea of raising the school leaving age from 14 to 15."
>
> "Yes I know," she said, "I just heard it on the wireless."
>
> "But they shouldn't be allowed to do this sort of thing," I said (as if it were her fault) "I'm supposed to be finishing school in July. Now I'll have to stay on until December. It's just not fair. That's another four months I've got to wait before I can get a job!"
>
> "You're talking like it's a jail sentence, "stop wishing your life away," she said.
>
> "I'll stop wishing my life away the day I leave school, when I've got myself a job," I said, "When I'm bringing home a wage packet every Friday."

I was not in any way looking forward to spending **another** four more months sitting at home listening to the boring old wireless every night while my brothers and sisters get ready to go out somewhere. Being told to look away while my sisters Elsie and Muriel pull up their skirts, so my mother can paint their legs with some stuff called Leg-Tan. This was to make people think they were wearing real nylon stockings. Nor was I looking forward to seeing our Franky gawping at himself in the mirror wondering what the other six wonders of the world were up to.

Roll on December the 22nd, my last day in school!

I continued to deliver newspapers for Mrs. Story right up until it was time for me to leave school. It was around that time she told me she was thinking of selling up. She said she was getting too old to be running a shop. I think she was well into her eighties by then. She'd begun to look tired and weary, taking twice as long to mark-up the newspapers, and sometimes even giving people the wrong change. It was not very long after that we heard Mrs. Story had passed away peacefully in her sleep.

LIVERPOOL EDUCATION COMMITTEE

MEMORANDUM

From

HEAD TEACHER,

DEPARTMENT

SCHOOL

To

Liverpool, Dec 22 19[illegible]

Raymond [illegible] has attended the school for the past four years.
He is of average ability and is careful and neat in appearance and in the execution of his school work. Regular and punctual in his attendance he has always shown himself truthful and honest.

[illegible]

My final school report

Dad Wants A Doctor In The Family

Dateline: 22nd December, 1948.

Mr. Haley, the science teacher, shouts at Wally Fairchild for smoking in the school yard. He tells him to get off the premises and go out into the world and make something of himself. Wally, who's never progressed much beyond reading the Beano and the Dandy, who's always been at the bottom of the class in every subject, and who's basically, got shit for brains gives him the V sign. Not with just one hand, but with both hands, and tells him to mind his own 'effing business. He says he's left school now so he can do what he likes.

Mr. Haley grabs him by the scruff of the neck and drags him through the gates and out into the middle of the street.

Wally shouts back at the teacher through the railings, telling him how much he's hated going to school. He says all the teachers, including him need their canes shoving up their backsides. He tells him he wouldn't be a teacher for all the tea in China.

Wally (who a few years later on finishes up residing in Walton jail at Her Majesty's Pleasure) and I are the same age; fifteen and a quarter; the only two pupils in our school that are leaving today. I don't like school either but I don't keep going on about it like Wally does. Anyway, I don't have anything to do with him or his family 'cos trouble follows them around where ever they go. Most of his brothers have been in jail at some time or another. Dad says Wally's brothers take after their father, that he's worse than the lot of them. He says Wally's Dad is never out of The Crown pub getting blind drunk and looking for fights. He says he's had more fights than John Wayne.

Wally says he's not tramping up and down any streets begging for jobs, he's joining the Merchant Navy so he can see the world. He says his Dad's already agreed to sign the papers. I want to tell him it's probably because his Dad and his Mum can't wait to get rid of him, but I decide it's best to keep that thought to myself.

I tell Wally I'd like to join the Merchant Navy and see the world, but my Dad says I wouldn't last five minutes on a ship, that they'd have me scrubbing the decks from morning 'till night. And he should know because he used to work on the fishing trawlers before the war.

Wally says my Dad doesn't know what he's talking about; that he's talking through the back of his head. The Merchant Navy is nothing like what he says it is, nothing like getting tossed around in a grimy fishing trawler all day long. Dad says Wally Fairchild doesn't know his arse from his elbow. That he's still as thick as the day he first started school, just like the rest of his family. That's when Dad starts lecturing me about getting a proper job, a trade, and not to listen to the likes of Wally Fairchild. He says it's the only way to ensure my future prosperity; otherwise I'll never get anywhere in life. I'll always be struggling to survive - penny pinching all the time - living from hand to mouth. Always worrying if I'll have enough money to buy a bag of coal or pay the rent.

Neither my brothers nor I had the slightest interest in anything connected with the medical profession, which is what Dad always wished for. He tried on numerous occasions to get at least one of us interested in the medical profession, but always failed. In fact, he took the bus into town one day and spent a fairly large chunk of his hard earned money on a giant sized picture of a human skeleton, a black board and easel, and some expensive medical books. All in preparation for what became twice weekly two hour lessons on Anatomy and Physiology. As much as I disliked those long two hour lessons in the parlor, I tried really hard not to show it. I didn't want to disappoint my Dad, especially after him spending all that money.

I had no interest in learning about the structure of the human body. Not the slightest interest in knowing how many bones there are, or how many pints of blood flow through my veins each and every day, (as long as it does keep flowing of course). To put it more plainly, my father's lessons on Anatomy and Physiology (while peripherally entertaining) had no relevance to my future goals in life.

"If any of you boys are interested, I can quite easily get you a job in Broadgreen Hospital, where I work," he would always say at the beginning of each lesson. "It's steady work and it's a very interesting profession - a job for life, you could say."

No one speaks - we just sit quietly with our pencils and note pads on our knees staring up at the picture of the skeleton hanging in front of the fire-place.

"Anyone know the name of this bone?" Dad asks, pointing his stick at the upper part of the skeleton's leg.

Quick as a flash, Stan's hand shoots into the air.

"Dad, Dad! I know the answer. It's the Femur, the largest bone in the human body."

"Verrrry good Stan," Dad says, "Gooood boy."

"I know most of them now Dad," Stan says boastfully, "I've been reading the medical books you bought us; they're really interesting."

"Verrrry good Stan," Dad says, moving his stick to the skeleton's knee-cap. "Now let's go to Raymond, what about this one I'm pointing at, Ray?"

"Ermmmm."

"Come on now, you must know this one - it's one of the easiest."

Without taking his eyes off Dad, Stan nudges me with his elbow and with a slight nod of the head beckons me to look down at the note pad on his knee. He's scribbled the word HUMOROUS in big bold letters across the page. Albert sees it and immediately covers his mouth with his hand to stop himself from laughing out loud.

"I know it Dad, I know it Dad," he shouts, "I know the answer."

"Let Raymond answer," Dad says, let's see if he knows."

"Well Raymond, do you know the name of this bone I'm pointing at?" Dad asks.

"Yes, Dad, I think it's the humorous!"

Albert and Stan lose control and start laughing making Dad lose his temper and get very annoyed. He's just spent a tidy lump of money on two very expensive leather backed medical books for us all to study, and I have to come up with a brain farting answer like Humorous.

I want to kill my brother for deliberately giving me the wrong answer, but fortunately for him it's not the right time. Suffice to say, as much effort as he put into it and as hard as my father tried, he failed to inspire any of his sons to become even remotely interested in the medical profession.

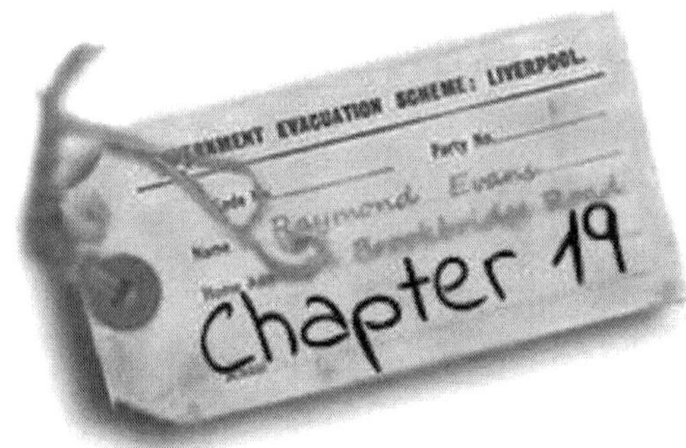

Dish Washer to Cake Decorator

Dateline: 7th JANUARY, 1949.

"There's an opening for an apprentice pastry chef in the State Restaurant where I work," Albert told me, when he arrived home from work. "They need someone right away. Are you interested? Don't think they've advertized the job yet."

"Yes, I am," I said. "Why, do think they'll take me on?"

"I think so; he said, "I'll ask if I can bring you in on Monday for an interview."

Dateline: 10th January, 1949.

“I couldn’t get to sleep thinking about that Italian head chef fella you kept going on about last night - him I've got an interview with today."

"What's that supposed to mean?"

"Well, the way he walks around the kitchen bawling and shouting at everyone like he's Mussolini himself. I mean, is he **really that bad**?”

“It's just the way he is,” Albert says, “he’s an Italian, that’s how Italians are. They’re very excitable people. Don’t worry about it.”

"As long as he's not one of those people who likes looking over your shoulder every few minutes; watching every move you make – I had enough of that in school."

“I told you, he hardly ever comes into the ‘veg’ kitchen where I work, or the pastry kitchen for that matter.”

"I don't remember you telling me that."

"You don't remember because you kept interrupting me before I had time to answer your first question."

"Like what?"

"Like how many chefs work in the main kitchen. How many work in the Pastry Kitchen? Are you allowed a break? How long for? Do you get paid overtime for working on Sundays, how much? In fact you've not stopped asking questions ever since we first got on **this** bus."

“Well, **do you know** how many people work in the pastry kitchen? You still haven't told me.”

"I **have** told you. There were three people working in the pastry kitchen until just a week ago, now there's only two - the chef and a washer-upper.”

"What happened to the other person, did he get the sack?"

"I don't know. And it was a She not a He."

"What's his name again?"

“Who's name?"

"The Italian’s name, him that’ll be interviewing me."

"Luigi Martinelli."

"Luigi what?

"Never mind. I'll tell you later. Come on, this is where we get off."

Its twenty minutes before ten when we step off the bus. The State Restaurant (one of the few buildings in the city centre spared from severe bomb damage) is just a block away on the other side of the busy thoroughfare of Dale Street. We enter the building by way of the Goods/ Employees entrance halfway along a narrow cobblestone side street.

After punching his clock card and telling the man in the office who I am, and that I'm here for a job interview, Albert leads the way down two flights of stairs, along a corridor to the employee’s changing rooms. Once he's changed into his chef whites we hurry back up stairs and head for Mr. Martinelli's office.

Its five minutes before the hour when we enter an unbearably hot kitchen.

"That's Luigi's office at the far end," Albert says, "but I don't think he's in yet; can't see any light on."

"What should I do, Al, should I just wait here?"

"No, go and wait outside his office."

"Do you think he'll mind if I take my jacket off, I'm sweating like a pig already?"

"No, he won't mind. Just sling it over your arm, he won't say anything."

"Are you sure? I mean he might......."

"Oh my God Ray, will you STOP worrying, he's not going to say anything - alright?"

"Okay, okay. It's just that I'm a bit nervous that's all."

"Don't forget to let me know how you get on," Albert says as he scurries off to his work bench in the 'veg' kitchen. Okay?"

"Okay, Al."

The beads of sweat that have been oozing out of my forehead while waiting for Mr. Martinelli to show up, have now found their way into the corners of my eyes making them sting. He unlocks the door to his office and invites me inside.

"Wharra your name?" He asks, lowering his large frame into the wide leather chair behind his desk.

"Raymond Evans, sir."

"How old?"

"Fifteen sir."

"You wanna-be-a chef-a-like-a your brother, no?"

"Yes, sir."

"You work-a hard like-a-him you can-a- start-a-work tomorrow, okay?"

"Tomorrow?"

"Yes, tomorrow, okay?"

"Yes. Thank you very much."

“Same-a wages as a-your brother, two pounds four-a-shillings and-a-sixpence, okay?"

"Yes sir. Thank you!"

"Good-a-boy. You come-a- weeth-a-me, I take-a you to meet-a-my brother Georgio."

Chief pastry chef Georgio Martinelli is busy decorating the bottom layer of the largest wedding cake I've ever seen in the whole of my life. Luigi taps him on the shoulder wanting to know where the washer-upper has got to - why is he not at his sink.Georgio, looks pretty irritated by his brother's interruption. He stops, turns around and says:

"Maybe he go to the toilet or maybe he go smoke a cigarette," I don’t-a-know, am-a-too busy to watch everything."

"A smoke?" Lugi screams. "Who tell him go for a smoke? Mamma-mia, he only just-a start-a work and he wanna smoke all-a-ready."

Luigi bounds across the kitchen like a mad elephant, opens the door to the goods delivery yard and spots the washer-upper (a pasty-faced twenty year old) seated on top of a dust bin rolling himself a fat cigarette. Luigi creeps up behind him.

"Warra you theeenk-a you do," Lugi shouts, snatching the tin rolling machine out of his hand. "Theees time I give-a-you the sack. No-a-more chances. Get out now! You donna work here anymore."

The washer-upper leaps up and follows Luigi back into the kitchen pleading for his job, apologizing profusely, saying it won't ever happen again. But Luigi's not having any, not this time. Luigi simply points to the door and tells the washer-upper to go wait outside his office for his cards and his money.

The washer upper puts his hands together like he's about to pray, "Please, please Mr. Martinelli, I've got a wife and two kids to support." Luigi pays no heed and tells him he should have thought about that before. That it's not the first time this has happened. Realizing all hopes of talking his boss around have now completely evaporated. The washer-upper unties his black rubber apron from around his waist, flings it to the floor at Luigi's feet, grabs his coat from the back of the door and on his way out of the kitchen, tells Luigi exactly where he can stick his lousy stinking job.

As if reading my mind, Luigi turns to me and asks if I'd like to start work right away.

"You mean washing pots and pans?"

"Just-a for two days, Luigi says, "maybe three - no more."

"But I'm in the wrong clothes to wash pots and pans. Can I start tomorrow instead?"

"Donna worry about-a-your clothes," Luigi says, "you wait-a-here, I fix-a-you up weeeth-a nice-a-new chef uniform."

He hurries off down stairs to the store room returning a few minutes later with a chef's jacket, a pair of blue check cotton trousers slung over his arm and my brother Albert at his side.

"You go weeeth-a-your brother to changing room, he says, "he show-a you where to put-a-your-a clothes, okay?"

"He's sacked the washer-upper," I tell Albert, as we make our way to the changing room. "That's why he wants me to start right away. What do you think I should do? I don't know whether to trust him or not."

"Take it," he says, "it's only till they get a new washer-upper. He has already told you that, right?"

"Well, yes he has, but.........."

"But what? What's wrong with you now? You're acting like you've just lost a ten-bob note and found a penny."

"I just hope he keeps his word, that's all. Don't want to go around telling people I wash pots and pans for a living, do I?"

"He **WILL** keep his word. Georgio will make sure of that."

"Georgio? What makes you say that?"

"Because he's desperate for an assistant - he needs help and Luigi knows that."

"Well I just hope you're right."

"I am right. Now you better start getting changed, otherwise you'll have Luigi down here looking for you."

"Okay. Where do I put my clothes?"

"You can put them in here with mine," Albert says, unlocking the metal door to his locker. "Just remember to fasten the padlock before you leave."

Minutes later I'm back in the kitchen fully clad in my new chefs uniform and long black rubber apron. I'm staring down at the mountain of greasy pots and pans trying very hard to console myself with Luigi's promise of being a washer-upper 'just' for one day - or maybe two.

Fortunately, as things turned out, my internship as a washer-upper came to an abrupt end the very next morning. I couldn't believe my eyes when I walked into the kitchen. There she was staring quietly at her reflection in Georgio's office window tying the thick rubber apron around her waist, a big plump middle-aged lady who was either deaf or didn't have the manners to answer when I said good morning to her.

"Are you the new washer-upper?" I ask in a much louder voice.

"No," she yells back, "I just like wearing rubber aprons - **okay**?"

Just then Georgio storms into the kitchen pointing to his office beckoning me inside.

"Betty already work-a-here," he says, in a low voice, "she a waitress. She work here a long-a-time, maybe twenty years I theeenk."

"She doesn't look too happy with herself," I tell him."What's wrong with her?"

"She not-a very happy today, Luigi take waitress job from her and give her washer-upper's job instead. You put-a-this hat on" he says, "you start-a-work with me now. You wanna-be a good-a-pastry chef, I **teach** you to be-a-good-a-pastry chef, okay?"

"Yes, okay, thank you very much."

In the weeks and months that followed Georgio taught me how to make crispy pancakes, pastries, deserts and later (for the traditional and very popular afternoon teas) his famous petite-fours. He even picked up on my interest and taught me how to ice and decorate cakes to the extent I was able (a few years later) to decorate a cake for my sister-in-law's 21st birthday. Little did I know I would be required to resurrect those cake decorating skills five decades later when Lilian and I moved to live in the USA.

*****

After years of wearing hand-me-downs and cast-offs, my six shillings pocket money would enable me to afford my very first suit. I'd seen it in a Department Store window one Saturday morning when grocery shopping for my mother, a task that was handed to me simply because I was the only one in the family (other than my mother) who fully understood how the Ration Books worked.

It was the snappy looking navy blue pin stripe that took my eye. Very similar to the one Humphrey Bogart wore in one of his gangster films that I'd seen recently. I came out of Lipton's grocery shop carrying two heavy shopping bags, crossed over the road to the Department Store and went inside to check out the price.

"Nineteen shillings and eleven pence plus fifteen clothing coupons," the man said, "Or just two shillings a week over ten weeks, then the suit's all yours sonny."

"How much deposit would I need?" I asked.

"Your first payment of two shillings counts as your deposit,"

"Oh that's good and what about interest?"

"We only charge interest if you go over the ten weeks payment period."

"No interest at all?"

"Nope."

I came out of the store in raptures. In ten weeks-time I'll have my very first suit, bought with my own money. My days of wearing hand-me-down clothes would soon be over.

"Why did you buy it from Sturlas?" asked Albert, when I got back, "Mr. Alexandra sells suits, good ones as well."

"Mr. Alexandra, who's he?"

"The Tally-Man, you must have seen him? He calls every Friday evening around six o'clock."

"You mean him with that big fancy car?"

"Yes, that's him".

"I wouldn't buy anything from him."

"Why?"

"Because his stuff's way too expensive and Mum says he charges too much interest."

"How much interest does Sturlas charge?"

"None."

"None, how come?"

"Because they don't charge interest under ten weeks, that's why. You'll still be paying interest off your suit long after I've finished paying for mine. That's how Mr.

Alexandra can afford that big fancy car he drives around in; why everyone calls him the "never-never man".

Ten weeks later the sales clerk stuffs my final payment inside a tube-like canister and sends it whizzing across the store to the cash office, returning a few minutes later with my receipt folded neatly inside. He screws off the top takes out the receipt and slips it inside the carrier bag along with my suit.

I raced home very impatient to try it on.

State Restaurant Closes

Dateline: 24th September, 1949.

Looking back the sudden closure of the State Restaurant I believe was, mainly due to the general austerity and lack of money that was so prevalent after the war.

The closing of the restaurant meant both Albert and I were now out of work. The loss of both his and my wages worsened an already desperate situation. Mum was out of her mind with worry. Dad's, Elsie's, Muriel's and Frankie's wages wouldn't be enough to prevent the family from falling back into debt. Because of the rising cost of food, a half crown was needed just to cover the weekend bread bill. It was horrible having to watch my mother count the pennies trying to get through each week. Worrying whether there'll be sufficient money left over to pay the coal man and the milk man. She said the way things were looking she may have to pawn my new suit to help pay the food bills.

I asked Georgio if he knew of any other restaurants close by where I might get a job right away. He told me he knew of one but wasn't sure if I'd like it there. It's a different class of restaurant altogether, he said. Nothing like I'd been used to in 'The State.' It doesn't matter, I told him. Just give me the name and where it is.

> "It's the Exchange Station Hotel in Tithebarn Street," he said, "just a few minutes' walk from the State Restaurant. The head chef is a friend of mine. I'll give him a ring."

At least it was a chance at a job, and I might not have to go home and tell my mother I was out of work.

Pawn Shop Problem!

Dateline: 26th September, 1949.

Georgio was good to his word and made the call to his friend. He even gave me a letter of recommendation which I'm sure, was why I got the job at the Exchange Hotel, because the competition was stiff to say the least. The only trouble was; I did not really fancy working in such a small dingy kitchen preparing cheap uninteresting meals for train passengers. Worse still, my eight hour day would be broken into two four hour shifts, eight in the morning through twelve, then four in the afternoon through eight, but it was after all a job and I was very glad to have it.

I was put on a month's trial at thirty five shillings a week; a big drop from what I was getting at the state restaurant. It would have to do till I'm able to find something better, I kept telling myself. Albert, I found out later, got himself a job the very same day working for Hanson's Dairies. In view of the long journey home, the four hour break in the afternoon would have to be spent in the staff lounge, either listening to the wireless, reading a newspaper or risk losing my wages playing cards. Saturdays on the other hand were a little different. That was the day - on the stroke of twelve, I'd get changed into my suit and spend most of my four hour break, away from the restaurant. My first port of call was always Mirabell's Tea Rooms a few minutes' walk down the road. I never needed a menu. The waitress didn't even bother with her note-pad.

> "The usual?" she'd say, as I sat down at the table. "Two pork pies, mashed potatoes and peas, followed by a small dish of rice pudding and a nice hot cup of tea?"
>
> "Yes please, thank you."

And all for the very reasonable price of one shilling and sixpence. Those were the days. After that I'd either take a stroll down to the Pier Head and sit and watch the ferry boats on the River Mersey, or spend a couple of hours in one of the cinemas, anything to get away from the Exchange Hotel which I came to hate so much.

I ended up walking out on my job at the Exchange Hotel a few months later. The problems started with Freddy Gibbons the kitchen porter. His main duty was to collect the dirty pots and pans and other kitchen utensils that the chefs had been using, wash and dry them and get them back into use as quickly as possible. Freddy, a single, overweight, pot-bellied sixty year old was generally known for spending his four hour breaks upstairs in the Hotel Bar devouring several bags of crisps and consuming industrial quantities of alcohol.

It all started one Saturday afternoon, when I was sitting in the lounge waiting for the rain to ease off, so I could go for my usual Saturday stroll around town. Suddenly the door burst open and in staggered Freddy. Everybody stopped what they were doing - they'd seen it all before. They could see by the expression on Freddie's face he was looking for trouble, that he'd had 'one' too many. He stood in the doorway for a few moments swaying from side to side scanning the room with his blood-shot eyes, until he focused on the person he was looking for. He staggered over to where I was sitting, bent over until his nose was practically touching mine and said:

> "I see yer ma's managed to get yer fancy suit out of the pawn shop again then?"

I stood up shocked, stunned and horribly embarrassed. *How could he possibly know about my suit being pawned? I've never told anyone about that.*

> "Leave him alone," someone shouted "He's done nothing to you."

With that, everyone stood up to get a better view of what was going on. I could feel my face turning bright red as I tried pushing past 'drunken Freddy'.

> "Let me past," I said.

> "F * * * * * g make me,"

Freddy said, taking a bottle of beer out of his pocket and threatening to smash it over my head.

"Leave the kid alone," someone shouted, as he tried pulling him away.

Freddy ignored him like he wasn't there.

"Yer didn't know, did yer? He said, poking his boney finger in my chest. Yer didn't know I knew about yer little pawn shop secret?"

It was easy to tell by the expression on his face I hadn't a snowflake chance in hell of calming him down. I could tell it was the beer that was talking, and that he wouldn't be happy until he was beating the living daylights out of me. I had to do something quick before it was too late. So I made a tight fist and before Freddy realized what was happening, I was able to land it flat on his nose. The power behind the punch knocks his swaying body off balance forcing him backwards onto the floor.

Red faced and humiliated knowing that my "little pawn shop secret" was now out in the open, I dashed over to my locker for my raincoat and headed down the stairs to the Chef's office door to tell him I was leaving.

"Who is it?" he shouted, in his usual impatient tone, "I'm in the middle of my lunch."

"Can I have my cards please, I'm leaving."

"Leaving? What do you mean? What the hell for?"

"It's Freddy," someone shouts from behind. "He's drunk again. He threatened Ray with a beer bottle."

"I'll sack him right now," the chef says; "You don't have to leave just because of that drunken bastard."

"It won't make any difference," I told him, "I'm still leaving."

*****

I dreaded having to go home and tell my mother that I'd walked out on my job, and after only three months.

"I'm sorry Mum," I said, "I know we need the money but I just couldn't stay there any longer, not now everyone knows about my suit being pawned."

"That's alright," she said, "I can understand how you felt, but you shouldn't have hit him - that was wrong."

"Yes I know, but I felt so embarrassed in front of everyone. They were all standing there staring at me."

"You must have hit him pretty hard to knock him to the ground, a big man like that."

"It wasn't difficult, he was drunk and already off balance swaying all over the place."

"Well I think you're over sensitive about things like that. Probably because of the years of put downs from when we were evacuated. It's left you with a lot of insecurities that are still following you around."

“But how did he know about my suit being pawned, I’ve never told anyone about that?”

“It doesn’t take a lot of working out,” she said. “There are a lot of families like us. We’re all in the same boat, having to rely on the local pawn shop just to get by. Don’t forget, (like so many people) we’ve had to start over again, your Dad and I, we lost practically everything because of the damn war.”

“Yes, I know, but it’s still embarrassing!”

“But what I do not understand, is why this man was trying to pick a fight with you in the first place. You must have said or done something to set him off.”

“Yes I had, but it wasn’t until I was on my way home that I realized what it was. He was probably mad at me because I’d refused to loan him money last week, when he was losing at cards. Anyway, I was thinking of trying Hanson’s Dairies for a job, they’re always looking for people, according to Albert.”

“I don’t understand,” she said, “why go there? I thought you’d set your mind on becoming a pastry chef?”

“It’s good money, that’s why.”

“Yes I know, but it’s a back breaking job, lugging ten gallon cans of milk around all day. Albert will tell you that.”

“Yes, he told me, but it’ll do until I go in the Army next year.”

Boot Camp Blues

Dateline: 5th September, 1951.

I received notification from the Ministry of Defense, instructing me to report to the local recruiting office to sign up for my two year stint in the Army. Because of the Korean War national service had now been extended from Eighteen months to two years.

A week later, I received another notice instructing me to go for a medical examination to ensure I was fully fit for military service. This was followed by a short interview with the Military Interviewing Officer. In short, the MIO's job was to match each recruit to the Service most suitable to that person's skills and experience.

"The Royal Army Service Corps would really suit me fine," I tell him.

"Oh, is that so," he says, "So you've got it all worked out, have you?"

"Yes, that way I could get my driving license for when I come out just like my brother did when he was in the R.A.S.C. I mean, I've got to think about when I come out, haven't I? Getting myself a steady job and all that? Not that I intend to drive a lorry all my life, but it would be a start, don't you think?"

"And that's your reason for wanting to join the R.A.S.C?"

"Yes."

"What about the Royal Army Medical Corps," he asks, going over my papers.

"No, no. Definitely not the R.A.M.C. Don't fancy that one little bit. I'll stick to the R.A.S.C. but thanks all the same, I do appreciate you giving me a choice."

What a wazzock. What a complete dip-stick I was to think I was entitled to choose which of the services I wanted to join. No wonder he was smirking at me. That sort of thing just didn't happen in the days of National Service. They put you where they wanted to put you, end of story Mister, get on with it.

I was recounting the whole scene for Frank when I got home; he about bust a gut laughing.

"So you thought you were entitled to pick any regiment you fancied" he said, "is that what you're saying?"

"Well, yes," I said, "I mean it worked for you didn't it? They put you in the R.A.S.C. So why shouldn't it work for me?"

"But I didn't ask for any particular regiment, did I?"

"But you told me you did. You told me you asked to be put in the R.A.S.C. so you could get your driving license? It was the last thing you said as I was leaving the house this morning. Ask anyone here, they all heard you. "Don't forget to tell the man you want to go in the R.A.S.C." that's exactly what you said."

"I was joking!"

"Joking? Is that what you call it? Well look where it's landed me, in the bloody R.A.M.C."

*****

Dateline: 18th September, 1951.

My father reached up to the mantelpiece for the official government envelope that was wedged behind the clock.

"Your National Service papers from the Ministry of Defense," he said, "They arrived not long after you left for work this morning."

Inside was a one way train ticket to Euston Station in London, together with explicit instructions on how to get to the

Royal Army Medical Corps barracks at Crookham, in Berkshire. There was also a stiffly worded warning stating that if I failed to report, it will be considered desertion and as such would carry a very severe penalty. The look on my face told my father I was not looking forward to spending a tenth of my life in the army, least of all, in the Royal Army Medical Corps.

A work mate who'd recently been de-mobbed from the R.A. M.C. had told me what to expect. He told me that once my initial training was complete I'd more than likely finish up in some military hospital working on the wards, which as far as he was concerned, would undoubtedly be the worst job in the whole of the British Army. He said I'd be working with some crabby faced matron who because of the three 'pips' on her shoulders, thinks she's God Almighty. He said she'll have me running up and down the wards from eight in the morning 'til eight in the evening while she sits on her lazy fat arse dishing out orders.

"You've got to think ahead, you've got to think about when you come out," my father says, looking up from his newspaper.

"What do you mean?"

"Think about all the free medical tuition you'll gain. Hospitals are crying out for male nurses, every single day."

"Sorry Dad, but I'm not interested."

He shook his head and went back to his newspaper.

*****

Lime Street Station, one week later:

He slides the carriage door closed, tosses his suitcase onto the overhead luggage rack and flops down in the seat directly opposite where I'm sitting. A tall skinny lad who looks every bit the typical college type dressed in his double breasted blazer, grey flannels and a blue and red striped college tie.

"Excuse me," he says, in his posh upper-class accent, "sorry to interrupt your reading, but are you going to the same place as me, Crookham Barracks?"

"Yes I am; how did you guess?"

"That envelope sticking out of your pocket, I've got one of those damn things as well."

"Where are you from?"

"Blundell Sands, near Crosby," he says, reaching over to shake my hand. "Name's Pickles - Norman Pickles."

"Ray Evans - pleased to meet you."

"I'm not looking forward to this Army thing one little bit, are you?"

"No, I'm not," I said, "but......"

"Trouble is," he said, before I had time to finish, "We can't do a damn thing about it, can we? That's what I don't like. We have no damn say in the matter. Now if I had my way I'd......"

Norman stops in mid-sentence and stares at the man entering the compartment. He's a short tubby white haired distinguished looking gentleman who just so happens to be wearing the uniform of a Royal Army Medical Corps Major. Norman, deciding its best not to continue with the conversation, sits back and starts fidgeting with his government envelope, taking the papers out of his pocket, reading them and stuffing them back again.

I kept glancing over the top of my newspaper wondering how Norman was going to get through the next two years. It was easy to tell he'd led rather a pampered life. That he'd been mollycoddled by his 'Mummy and Daddy', as he later referred to them. It made me wonder what kind of person he'd turn out to be once he'd completed his two years National Service. Army life was widely known for quickly transforming the spoilt and wimpy into men. In other words, those who found it difficult, living under strict Army discipline.

We clamber onto the platform at Euston Station and are led to a canvas topped lorry waiting outside to take us to Crookham Barracks - a motley group of raw recruits ready to begin our very first day in the British Army.

I can still remember arriving at the camp and seeing Lance Corporal Callaghan standing to attention outside the Quarter Master's Store, his baton tucked under his arm. A fowl mouthed five foot dumpy little man who was about to have some of the raw recruits shaking in their boots, including Norman.

He led us inside where we were each issued an ill-fitting 'Best' uniform. An even worse-fitting second 'Best' uniform; a

'Best' pair of boots and a second 'Best' pair of boots which, despite microscopic inspection, I failed to see the difference. We were issued with a Physical Training (PT) kit as well as a one size beret that would have been far too big even for Humpty Dumpty's head. And last but not least, a mess-kit consisting of an enamel mug; a couple of metal Dixie cans and a set of metal eating utensils.

Later that day, after our regulation Army haircut (a very quick and definitely not stylish short back and sides) we were marched to a ramshackle thirty man wooden hut that had barely any heating, poor washing facilities and a row of smelly antiquated toilets.

Our eight weeks basic training began early the next morning on the parade ground, learning how to react to the drill Sergeant's very loud quick-fire commands; the very same day that poor Norman was put on a charge; the same day he had serious thoughts of deserting. Three weeks later, after numerous hours of hard square- bashing, Norman was still finding it a little tricky keeping in-step with the rest of us. Even marching in a straight line was a problem for lanky-legged Norman. It was no wonder the drill sergeant was always losing his temper with him. Norman simply didn't know his left foot from his right. I can see him now as I write, marching along with the drill Sergeant at his side screaming down his ear. Whenever I see John Cleese (of Monty Python fame) doing one of his Ministry of Silly Walks on TV, it never fails to remind me of the gangly legged Norman Pickles on that parade ground.

During field training, we were taught how to throw hand grenades at empty wooden buildings, dud ones that is, not real hand grenades. How to shoot and take care of our 303 Lee Enfield rifle by taking it to pieces, cleaning and putting it back together again. Norman's delicate stabbing technique at the 'straw filled enemy' does not go down too well with the drill sergeant.

> "It's not a piece of steak you're stabbing laddy," he shouts. "You're supposed to attack it, not tickle it man!" The meticulous attention to detail for some of the people in 'F' company was too much to take. I remember wakening up one morning and seeing the guy in the bunk opposite sitting on the side of his bed smoothing the toe-caps of his boots with the back of a teaspoon that he'd heated over a candle.
>
> "What's going on?" I said, "Its two o'clock in the morning."
>
> "Can't sleep, I need to get my kit ready for tomorrow's inspection. The Corporal said he'll put me on a charge if I don't get the wrinkles out of these toe-caps." The poor fellow was a nervous wreck. He was still at it when we came back from breakfast an hour later.

Regular barrack room inspections occurred once a week - kit inspections more frequently. If your kit or your part of the barrack room was not up to standard, strict punishment would follow. You would be confined to barracks for seven days doing menial jobs like spud bashing, weeding flower beds, picking up bits of paper, mopping and cleaning foul-smelling latrines. Or if you were really unlucky, cutting the grass outside the officer's mess, not with a lawn mower, but (and I'm not making this up) on your hands and knees using a pair of scissors.

Desertion was a common occurrence during the early days of basic training. Two of the men from our barrack room went AWOL (Absent without Leave) just four days after arriving at the camp. They were quickly picked up and brought back a few days later to be charged with desertion.

Norman would have been the third person to do a runner had he not been talked out of it by someone in the barrack room. His main reason for wanting to sneak off during the night, he told me, was the never ending torrent of abuse he was receiving every day from Lance Corporal Callaghan. I heard Norman whimpering under his blankets one night. A grown man crying for his mother I found hard to comprehend.

Eight weeks later. End of training:

Lance Corporal Callaghan stomps along the barrack room rubbing his fat stubby fingers across the tops of the lockers searching for minute particles of dust. He stops at

Norman's bed and tells him he's the worst recruit he's ever had to train. That he's pleased and overjoyed he won't have to look at his ugly face ever again. He tells Norman that if there was a special trophy for being put on a charge as many times as he had, he'd win it hands down.

I keep wondering what's inside the envelope the Corporal's carrying. Is it something to do with our postings? Because if it is, I wish he'd get on with it. We'd all like to know where they're sending us; the Far East, or the Middle East.

"Righty-ho you lot," he shouts,

"I'm going to read out these postings, once and only once, so open your lug-holes and listen carefully, I'm not going to stand here all day repeating myself. The sooner I see the back of your ugly faces, the better. So when I call out your name and posting, I want to hear you shout loud and clear, YES CORPORAL! DO - YOU - HEAR - ME?"

"YES CORPORAL!"

I listened carefully, wishing and hoping for either a Far East posting or if I were really lucky, a Home posting like my brother Stan was given a few years later. The place I did not want to be sent was the Middle East. Suffice to say, I did not get my wish.

"Private Evans - Middle East Posting, Canal Zone."

"YES CORPORAL!"

Troop Ships, Tents & King Tut

Dateline: February, 1952.

We sailed on the SS Empire Medway, a huge troop ship carrying some two thousand men. I remember standing on the deck looking down at the small crowd below waving and cheering as the ship began slipping away from its moorings. I noticed a lot of the lads were very excited at going overseas. All lured by the thought of the great adventures they'd have. Myself, I wasn't so sure, in fact, I was a little apprehensive knowing there was a very strong possibility I would finish up in the middle of the desert working on some hospital ward for the remainder of my national service.

Troop Ship Medway
(Img. courtesy of Suez Veterans Assoc.)

To relate this little tale of woe

Off to Egypt we must go

To desert sands ‘neath burning sun

Where heaven ends and hell’s begun

Port Said, Egypt:

We were transferred from the ship to a long line of lorries assembled on the quayside ready to take us (under armed guard) to a place called Fayid, which according to the map, was on the western shore of the Great Bitter Lake. The sun burned down on our shaky World War Two canvas top-lorry making it feel like we're sitting in an oven. It bounced its way along the rough and stony roads making the bone jolting long hot journey feel like it would never end.

It was mid-afternoon when the long convoy finally reached its destination - the Headquarters of Britain's Middle East Land Forces - our home for the next twenty months.

Three days later, I'm sent over to Fayid Military Hospital and put to work on the E.N.T. ward. Captain James is the matron in charge, a slim, stony faced, bad tempered, despicable little lady, who in my opinion would've been better suited to working for the Gestapo.

My busy eight hour day includes administering medicines. Taking temperatures and checking blood pressures. Putting drops up people's noses, in their eyes, and in their ears. Giving injections and sterilizing the needles, changing dressings, changing beds, mopping floors, and worst job of all, racing up and down the ward with smelly bed pans every few minutes. I'm kept going non-stop from eight in the morning 'till eight in the evening when it's time for the night shift to take over.

Fayid Camp as I recall, it remained pretty much the same throughout my time there. I left Egypt in 1953. (Image courtesy of www.StanleyBriggs.com)

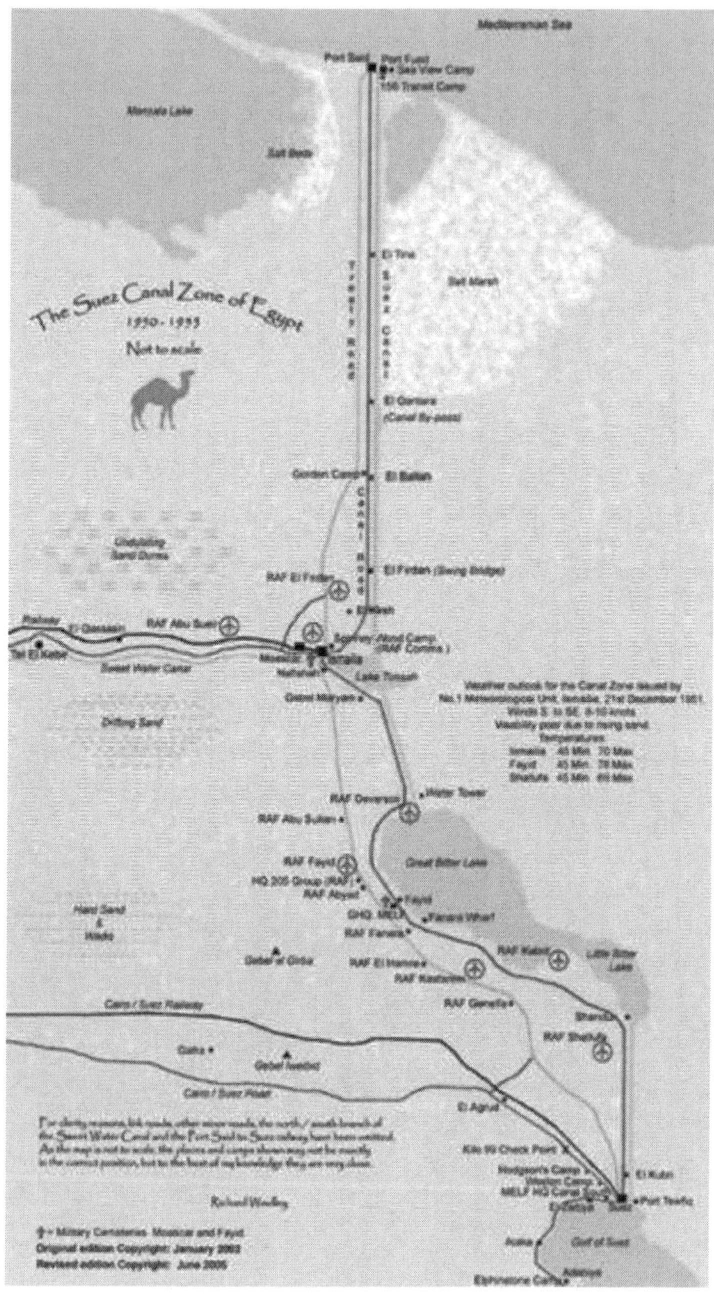

Map courtesy of Richard Woolley

www.suezveteransassociation.org.uk

Dateline: June, 1952.

The strong smell of sweating bodies, along with the intense strength sapping heat inside the twenty man 'night' tent makes sleeping during the day a near impossibility. Even with just my underpants and a thin cotton sheet covering my body, the baking mid-day sun makes it feel like I'm sleeping in a furnace. And that's not the worst of it.

The special "night tent" which is in a remote "out-of-the way" area of the camp reserved for night workers is heavily infested with giant armor piercing mosquitoes; millions and millions of the little blighters all with the same merciless quest for my blood. How the hell they're able to squeeze inside my supposedly impenetrable mosquito net is a mystery to be sure. I have to do something about it because they're driving me crazy. I no sooner squash one of the little blighters and another comes buzzing into the net. And so it goes on throughout the day as I desperately try to snatch a few minutes sleep before I have to get up and go back on duty.

Land of sweat and a shirt that stinks

Land of pyramids and land of sphinx

Sweat rash, foot rot, prickly heat

Aching hearts and blistered feet

Swarms of flies that buzz and bite

Mosquitoes zinging through the night

That's me on the right, taken with a pal at
Fayid, Egypt during my National Service

Working The Wards & A Visit From A VIP

Chalky White (the corporal in charge of the cook-house) and I became good friends in the short time we knew each other. Had it not been for this man, I'd have remained working on the hospital wards right up to my very last day in the army.

I asked him one day when we were alone if he would explain how he was able to get off the wards.

"Very difficult," he said, "took me nearly three months."

"Three months?"

"Yes, three months. Practically everyone you speak to wants to get off the wards."

“If it’s that difficult, how the heck did you do manage it?

“I just made a general nuisance of myself, kept complaining to the matron. Kept telling her how much I hated working on the wards, she didn’t like that much at all.

“What did she do?”

“She kept ignoring me at first until I began making things even more difficult for her.”

“Like what?”

“I got up to all sorts, like coming in late every morning, pretending I was sick. I kept the patients waiting for a bed-pan - that really got her goat, having to sit in her office listening to someone yelling for a bed-pan every few minutes. Trouble was; she knew exactly what I was up to; she knew I was trying my damndest to get off those wards.”

“What happened then?”

“She lost patience, put me on a charge and sent me in front of Colonel McNulty, which was just what I wanted.”

“So it was him that took you off the wards?”

“Yes. He put me on spud bashing from six in the morning until six in the evening. And that was seven days a week, no days off. Then one day, right out of the blue, I’m put in the kitchen to help with the cooking. Me a cook, can you believe that? Shorthanded is what they said. I don't have a clue about cooking; can't even boil an egg!"

"I don't understand? How come you finished up with two stripes in charge of the cookhouse?"

"Don't ask me, but that's what happened. I do know one thing though, it certainly wasn't Colonel McNulty's doing."

"Do you think it might work for me?"

"Don't know, do I? Like I said before, practically everyone I know wants off the wards."

"I'm not going to let that stop me. Anything would be better than working on those wards."

"Don't forget, Colonel McNulty could just as easily have had me going round the camp cleaning the latrines and digging holes to make new ones. Imagine doing that for the remainder of your time?"

"I'll take that chance. I'll start complaining to the matron first thing in the morning. I think I could get pretty good at it!"

Visit From A VIP:

One evening while sitting on the side of my bed tying my boot laces getting ready to go on night duty Sergeant Fielding comes barging into the tent shouting on top of his voice:

"Private Evans! Is Private Raymond Evans in here?"

"I'm over here sergeant," I shouted, raising my arm.

"Right, finish what you're doing and follow me to the Guard Room, and MOVE YOUR SELF!"

"Guard Room? I don't understand, what am I supposed to have done?"

"Don't ask me. All I know is that the Duty Officer has ordered me to get your body over to the Guard Room as quickly as possible. So you better move your bloody self."

"The Duty Officer, what's going on? I'm on night duty in half an hour."

"No you're not; your night duty starts at nine o'clock tonight, not eight. So stop your nattering and get a move on."

I was surprised (and so was the mouthy sergeant) when the guard room Duty Officer Captain Garfield stood up from his desk and pointed to a chair inviting me to sit down next to him. It must be bad news, I thought, this is not normal, something bad has happened at home.

"Don't look so worried, Private Evans," the D.O. said, "there's nothing wrong; you're not in any trouble."

"Then why am I here, sir, can you please tell me what's going on?"

The phone rang just as he was about to explain, so I had to wait while my mind ran riot thinking of every worst case scenario possible.

> ***Something must've happened at home, I thought to myself, something serious.***

He finished speaking, put the phone down and ordered me to follow him outside.

> "Stay here by the door under the light," he said, "and whatever you do, do **not** move from this spot."
>
> "Sir, can you please tell me what's going on?"
>
> "Don't forget," he said, ignoring my question, "When he gets here, you must come to attention and give him your best, smartest salute. I'll be looking for it."
>
> "Yes sir, I will, but..."

He raced on foot along the narrow dirt track up to the main gates about two hundred yards away, arriving at the same time the gates were beginning to open. There was a firestorm of activity as a jeep entered the compound. People were coming to attention and saluting all over the place. I started to wonder if Churchill himself was going to step out of the vehicle. I immediately fixed my eyes firmly on the jeep trying to focus on the person sitting in the back. But the Captain was speaking to the driver and blocking my view.

Then something very odd happened. The driver of the jeep not only swings his vehicle round to face the guard room, but leaves his engine running and his head- lights switched on.

> ***What the hell is he doing?*** I asked myself. ***Why's he gone and done that? The headlights are blinding me!***

It wasn't until the Captain and this mysterious VIP were just a few yards away from the guard room steps (when the jeep's headlights had been switched off) that I would finally discover who the other officer was. I could not believe my eyes when he stepped out of the shadows and I was able to see his face. There I was, standing smartly to attention, giving (as ordered) my smartest salute to none other than my own father.

> "How are you son?" he said quite casually. "How's life treating you?"

That was to be the most treasured and memorable moment I have of my father. He'd driven all the way from Port Said just to see me; quite a risky journey to say the least, considering all the hostilities that were still going on throughout the region at that particular time.

I felt so very proud of my Dad that day. Not only because he looked so smart in his white Naval Officer's Uniform, but seeing all those people coming to attention and saluting him, especially loud mouth sergeant Keating.

I stood there on the guardhouse steps thinking how far he'd come from the appalling poverty-stricken days he'd endured as a young boy - admiring his tenacity and never ending determination to make something of himself.

*****

Dateline: August, 1952 – Chalky's Got a Plan.

The likelihood of Chalky's plan ever working was diminishing rapidly, at least in my mind it was. I'd tried everything Chalky had suggested but nothing was working. In fact, I was pretty certain the matron knew exactly what I was up to. Then one day, right out the blue, she bursts onto the ward looking even angrier than usual, taps me on the shoulder and in her sternest voice says:

> "Private Evans: Stop what you're doing and get changed out of your whites immediately. Lt. Colonel McNulty wants you in his office right away, hurry up now, he's waiting for you!"

This is it, they're finally taking me off the wards!

I changed out of my hospital whites into my uniform and raced across the square. The company sergeant major was already stood to attention outside Lt. Colonel McNulty's tent waiting to quick-march me inside.

"Left-right, left-right, left-right, HALT! SAH! Private Evans, SAH!"

He's a balding pasty faced little man with multiple medal ribbons above his pocket.

"What's your problem Evans?" he says, "what is it you find so terrible about working in a hospital?

"I don't like hospital work sir, don't find it very interesting."

"I see," he says, still scraping the inside of his pipe.

"National Service or Regular soldier?"

"National Service sir."

"Just a two year soldier - I thought as much. You hate the army, right Evans? Just like most National Service men do!"

"No sir, I don't hate the army, in fact I think the army's okay. Everyone has to do their stint. It's the job I've been given. I'm just not cut out for nursing work sir."

He leaps up from his chair, slams his fist hard down on his desk and shouts in a very loud voice:

"WHAT WAS THAT YOU JUST SAID?

THE ARMY'S OK?

IS THAT ALL YOU CAN SAY ABOUT THE BRITISH ARMY?

THAT IT'S JUST OKAY!

The army's a damned good life; you take it from me sonny. Thirty six years I've been serving my country and I've loved every minute of it.

A man can really make something of himself in the British Army, Private Evans. It's the perfect future for a young man like you who doesn't have a trade behind him. Good God man what's wrong with you?"

"Yes sir! Don't know sir! Sorry sir."

Oh God! I can't think straight, can't spit out platitudes fast enough, I'm really done for now.

He's shaking his head, clearly exasperated with my complete lack of interest in being or remaining in the R.A.M.C.

After shuffling the papers around on his desk he finally comes across the one he's been looking for:

"Right then Evans," he says, with a hint of joy on his face, "I'm posting you to 50 M.C.E departing at precisely 0-600 hrs tomorrow, so be outside the guardhouse with your kit. AND don't you dare be late!"

"Yes Sir."

"Oh! And one more thing Evans, do you know anything about this place, 50 M.C.E?"

"No sir. Never heard of it"

"It's a Military Correction Establishment I'm sending you to. You'll be doing menial jobs like cleaning out latrines and picking up paper around the camp - a general dog's body, if you like."

"Yes sir."

"It's just outside Moascar."

"Yes sir."

"Not far from Ismailia, right there where I'm pointing my finger. Can you see it, right there on the map?"

"Yes sir, I can see it."

"It's a squalid dirty little Hole. A place where people live in mud huts and bathe themselves in the smelly liquid latrine they call the Sweet Water Canal. Not the kind of place I'd choose to serve out the remainder of my time, I don't mind telling you. In fact, with all the trouble that continues to flare up out there in the middle of the desert, it wouldn't surprise me if the entire area will be out of bounds until after your national service is done. It certainly has been for the past few months. That can only mean one thing Private Evans; you won't be allowed outside the camp gates when an 'out of bounds' ruling is in force. You'll be locked inside, twenty four hours a day; just like you were an inmate yourself."

"Yes Sir."

"You do know this is a punishment posting I'm giving you, Private Evans?

“Yes sir.”

“You’ll be stuck in that God forsaken shit-hole for the remainder of your National Service!”

“Yes sir.”

“Well, do you have anything to say for yourself?”

“No sir.”

“You can still change your mind and go back on the wards. There’s nothing wrong with the job you were doing, looking after the sick. You should have been proud of what you were doing, not complaining all the damn time – you should be honored to be serving in the Royal Army Medical Corps!”

“Yes sir.”

“I’m giving you one last chance to remain working here on the wards Evans, so what’ll it be then? Do you want to stay?”

“No sir, no thank you sir.”

“Idiots, that’s what they send me, idiots! You leave at 0-600 hours sharp!”

“Yes sir.”

“That’ll be all Sergeant Major, get him out of my sight!”

My Dad George Evans. Sr.

Punishment Posting

My first glimpse of 50 M.C.E as I stepped from the vehicle, was the two-man Bren-gun emplacement dug-in, directly beneath its high thick wooden gates.

It was a scene that took me back to a film I once saw featuring a German prisoner of war camp. I stood for a moment watching the vehicle that brought me disappear into the distance, my kitbag propped up against my legs and my rifle slung over my shoulder. *What the hell have I got myself into? What kind of place has that man sent me to?*

The hot bumpy journey from Fayid to Moascar had been made worse by the impending sand storm that could be seen brewing over the horizon. The air was 'still' and muggy making it difficult to breathe properly. Looking up at the lofty guard tower, looming high above the barbed wire fencing, made me feel as if I was a convict about to begin a long prison sentence.

Main Gate Moascar Garrison (Img. SuezCanalZone.com)

"Wait over there," the guard shouted, "someone will be out shortly to check you in."

Twenty sweltering minutes later the guard house door swung open and out came a weary, sweat drenched, heavily built Staff-Sergeant holding a clip board in his hand.

"Name?"

"Evans."

"Evans what?" he says, pointing his finger at the three stripes on his arm, "Who do you think your speaking to? It's Sergeant when you speak to me, and don't you forget it."

"Sorry Sergeant, I wasn't thinking."

"First name?"

"Raymond, Sergeant."

"Number?

"22604253, Sergeant."

"Right, wait over there away from the gates and don't move. Captain Morris is on his way. He'll be here in a few minutes."

"Would you mind if I wait inside the guardhouse, it's sweltering out here. As you can see I'm still in full winter kit."

"Yes I do mind Private Evans; it's a guard house not a bloody waiting room?"

Gun Post Near Moascar Garrison (Img. SuezCanalZone.com)

Captain Morris, the medical officer for the camp arrived a few minutes later in a military driven jeep, a tall good looking man in his mid-thirties. He's a National Service recruit just like me, except that he has three pips on his shoulders. He doesn't salute but surprisingly offers me a firm friendly handshake instead, and asks me to follow him to the Medical Inspection Room (MIR) which is situated directly behind the guard hut. He introduces me to Brian the N.C.O. in charge.

"The Corporal's time is nearly up," Captain Morris says, "he'll be leaving for the UK shortly which means you'll be running things here then. Do you think you can manage that Evans?

Running things, what the hell's going on? McNulty never mentioned anything about me running a Medical Inspection Center!

"Erm, yes sir," I answer, still mystified as to what is happening, "Sure I'll be able to run things, no problem at all sir." I said, hoping to sound convincing.

"Your training has included administering injections, correct?"

"Yes sir."

"Good, that'll make things a lot easier for me. The rest is quite easy, much easier than working on those wards, I'm sure you'll agree"

"Yes sir."

"We've got the R.E.M.E. camp down the road to look after as well as two other smaller camps in the area, so I'm kept fairly busy. But I will be dropping by each morning, usually around eight in time for the morning sick parade to check if you need stocking up on anything in the medical cabinet. So if you have any questions before I leave, please fire away."

"No sir. I don't think so, not right now, anyway."

"Well that's it then Evans, I'll be off. It looks like we're going to get along just fine, cheerio old chap!"

"Cheerio sir."

"What a nice guy," I tell Brian, "Is he always like that?"

"Yes he is. He's a national service man just like you and me, don't forget. He hates the army. He can't wait to get back home, to get back to his family practice in Yorkshire."

"I'm finding it a bit hard to take it all in," I confess to Brian, "everything's happening so fast. I can't understand why I've been given the job of running the M.I. Room when I'm supposed to be on a punishment posting."

"It looks like someone's made a mistake," Brian says. "Captain Morris was told an N.C.O. would be taking over the M.I. Room. In fact, he should have been here two weeks ago so I could teach him the ropes."

"I'm sure you're right. I think there has been a mistake. Lt. Colonel McNulty didn't mention me taking charge of an MI Room, that's for sure. In fact, he told me I'd be spending the rest of my national service cleaning out latrines!"

"Well I hope for your sake he doesn't find out."

"You're not thinking of telling anyone, are you Brian, like Captain Morris for instance? I mean, I've no problem running the MI Room, that doesn't bother me in the slightest. Actually, it'll be a sight easier than working those wards in Fayid Hospital."

"No, of course I'm not. And anyway, why would I, why would it matter to me? I'm leaving shortly. I've done my time in this place, thank God."

*****

Medical Inspection Room:

The remainder of the day was spent going over the daily routine that Captain Morris had asked Brian to type up in preparation for the expected N.C.O. taking over. The afternoon on the other hand was taken up finding my way around the camp.

08:00 hrs:

Sick parade inmates marched to MI center, wait outside until MO is ready to inspect.

Medications prescribed by MO

Medications Administered by NCO.

09:30 hrs:

Clean MI room

Inventory medications

Prepare requests for review and submission to MO next day.

Prepare sick report for Col. Bellamy.

12:00 hrs:

Deliver sick report to Col. Bellamy's office.

15:00 hrs:

Treatment of inmate injuries post assault course.

As it turned out, the afternoons were the busiest part of my day. The camp was a former prisoner of war camp from WWII. After the war it had been turned into a Military Corrective Establishment. The "British Army" inmates had been found guilty of one or more crimes and subsequently found themselves "serving their time" in 50 MCE. The entire focus seemed to be on making their lives as miserable as possible. Probably to ensure they'd have absolutely no desire ever to return.

Every day in the afternoon heat, the inmates would be put through an extended assault course, twice as long; and ten times more challenging than any I'd endured in basic training. They would line up outside the Medical Center, hot, sweaty and totally exhausted waiting to have the rope burns on their hands "treated" with gentian violet – which if you've ever experienced that on an open wound, you'll have some idea how much it really stings.

*****

Mosquito Killing Maverick:

It was some weeks after arriving at the camp that Lance Corporal Huxley came into my tent one evening holding something in his hands.

"Do you know what this is?" he asked, opening up his hands.

"A Chameleon?"

“Yes,” he said, “That’s right, and it’s yours if you want him. My time’s up and I’m leaving for home tomorrow, so I don’t need him anymore.”

“Thanks,” I said, “but what would I want with a Chameleon?”

“To keep the bloody mosquitoes and flies away,” he said, “what do yer think?”

“Oh, I see. Can I hold him?”

“No, not if you don’t want him. I’ve had him a long time. I want someone to look after him like I have.”

“I do want him - I just wasn’t thinking.”

“Right then, he’s all yours as long as you promise to look after him. Cheerio!”

“Hey, hang on a minute. Where about in the tent do you suggest I keep this little fella?”

“Anywhere you to want during the day, but he’s best next to your mosquito net during the night. You won’t be bothered with mosquitoes anymore, not with him around, I can promise you that. Any more questions, I’m in a hurry, got to get back to packing my things.”

“No, and thanks for giving me first chance.”

“That’s ok, all the best then.”

“Thanks, and all the best to you too, you lucky sod, wish it was me going home.”

all I want is a peaceful world and a pork pie!

*****

Six months have gone by and I still can't get over how lucky I've been to have finished up with such a cushy number. I'm practically my own boss. This job I've been given, running the MI Room has to be without doubt, one of the cushiest numbers in the whole of the British army. To top that, Colonel Bellamy has now promoted me from Lance Corporal to full Corporal. What a nice guy he's turned out to be. Two stripes on my arm and all I'm doing is handing out aspirins, sticking needles in people's arms, bandaging cuts, and painting gentian violet on rope burns!

> "You're doing a jolly good job Evans," he says whenever he sees me, "Keep it up boyo."

Best of all; due to the promotion my weekly wage has gone up from forty shillings to forty six shillings a week. There's nothing to do around here and precious little to spend it on so I save about thirty shillings each week and put it into my P.O.S.B (Post Office Savings Bank) account for when I come out. That leaves me with roughly sixteen shillings spending money, which mostly goes on cigarettes, a couple of beers in the NAFFI, Oh, and I slip the Dobie (the laundry man) a few extra piaster's so he'll do a good job on my KD's (Lightweight Khaki Drill uniform).

The Naffi at Moascar Garrison (Img. SuezCanalZone.com)

Working it all out, I should have about £100 - £120 saved up by the time my two years are up. Which according to my calculations (the one that's on my make-shift -tent-wall-calendar I religiously track every night) is in 35 weeks, three days and seven hours – give or take a few hours. All in all, other than the heat and the boredom, there's one little niggling problem that keeps bothering me, and that's Colonel Bellamy. He wants me to sign on for another three years. I wouldn't mind so much if he just asked every now and then, but it's every time he sees me.

Like for instance when he's in my tent doing his daily camp inspection, or when I'm handing in the daily sick report. Mind you, to be fair to the old man, it's partly my own fault. I mean, I have sort of been giving him the wrong impression, by telling him I do "like" being a soldier - a grave error of judgment on my part. But what else am I supposed to say? I had learned my lesson with career Army Colonels when I ticked off McNulty, so I don't want to upset Bellamy now, do I? Especially not after him putting two stripes on my arm!

"So what do you think of the army then, Boyo?" He's Welsh you see. That's how the people speak in Wales to any male person, young or old.

"I'm enjoying it sir"

"That's what I like to hear Corporal. It's a dammed good life, isn't it boyo?"

"Oh yes sir, certainly is"

"Still haven't made your mind up yet then, about signing on?"

I pray my thoughts aren't evident across my face because they're now screaming

"You're entering the realms of fantasy now mister."

"Errr, no sir, not just yet, but I have been giving it some serious thought. I've written to my Mum & Dad to ask their advice about it though" I told him, hoping it may buy me a few weeks peace and quiet.

Fakers, Smokes & Mirrors?

Dateline: Spring, 1953.

It was in the early hours when one of the inmates began complaining about pains in his stomach.

"You need to come over to the compound," the guard said, shaking me out of a deep sleep. "Sorry to wake you mate, but it's looking pretty serious. It's private Crowe - he's rolling all over the floor moaning and groaning."

"Private Crowe? Are you sure he's not just putting it on again? You know what he's like."

Private Crowe was known for two things, faking illnesses and numerous failed attempts to escape.

"No I don't think he is putting it on," the guard says, "not this time anyway. He's holding his stomach like he's been stabbed. I think it could be a bad bout of dysentery he's got."

"OK. I'll be over as quick as I can, just need to throw my clothes and boots on and grab a pack of dysentery tablets from the medical cabinet."

I noticed on reaching the compound that one of my boot laces was undone, so before opening the gates to let myself in, I bent down to re-tie it.

"HALT! WHO GOES THERE?" the voice rang down from the guard tower "IDENTIFY YOURSELF."

"Whoa! Stop pointing that bloody gun at me," I shouted, "It's me, Corporal Ev..."

"STAND FAST AND GIVE YOUR NAME, RANK AND NUMBER!"

"IT'S ME! IT'S ME!" I shouted, a bit louder. "DIDN'T YOU HEAR WHAT I JUST SAID? STOP POINTING THAT GUN AT ME. I'M CORPORAL EVANS FROM THE MEDICAL CENTRE! SOMEONE IS SERIOUSLY ILL IN THERE."

"Sorry Corporal, I didn't recognize you."

"That's ok, it's my own fault I suppose; I should have picked somewhere else to tie my boot lace. By the way, did I hear you shove a bullet up the breech just then?"

"Yes, I'm sorry, but that's what we're supposed to do; there have been a lot of break-ins lately, people coming under the wire trying to break into the Armory. The sergeant told us to always push one up the spout as a warning to anyone we don't recognize."

"Yes, but just tell me, you didn't have your finger on the trigger as well, did you?"

"Nah" he answered a little too casually, "My finger wasn't anywhere near the trigger. I got a bit panicky, that's all. Not the smartest place to decide to check your boot laces though eh Corp, at the bottom of the tower and all?"

All this time, Private Crowe is lying flat out on his bed with his hands tucked behind his head, all calm and relaxed.

"What's going on?" I ask the sergeant when I enter the tent, "He looks alright to me."

"There's nothing wrong with him," the sergeant says, "he's just been putting it on."

"Maybe, maybe not," I tell him, "but just to be on the safe side, I'll go back and get him something to settle his stomach."

Private Crowe eyes me a little skeptically when I get back.

"I think it's passed off now," he says, his eyes fixed on the medicine bottle, "can't feel the pains anymore."

"Well, drink it anyway," I tell him, handing him the glass. "You never know, it may come back."

"Cor blimy, what **IS** that stuff," he says, clutching at his throat, "tastes bloody awful."

"That's the only medicine that'll clear the colon faster than anything I know," I tell him. "In about half an hour, you'll be sorry you ever complained about pains in your stomach. In fact, that stuff you've just drank is so powerful, in about twenty minutes or so, you'll be frightened to even sneeze."

Losing his two-a-day cigarette ration was too much for Private Crowe. Three days wouldn't have been so bad, (which is what he was expecting) but to be without a 'smoke' (as he put it) for **two whole weeks** was going to be absolutely unbearable. He begged and pleaded with Colonel Bellamy to give him another chance. The Colonel showed no sympathy.

"Consider your-self very lucky it's not longer," he told Private Crowe, "next time it'll be four weeks."

Private Crowe was frustrated at losing his cigarette ration for such a long, merciless, and cruel period. He clearly felt it was an overly stringent punishment from the Colonel, to say the least. His chosen course of action was to immediately attempt yet another escape. This time, he planned to make it all the way to Port Said, where he intended to stow-away on a ship back to England.

The last time he tried to escape, he failed miserably. He was nabbed before he even got a hundred yards from the camp. However, this next time was going to be quite different, he told his fellow inmates. He planned to make his escape when the next sand storm hit. He knew he would be on road sweeping duty outside the camp with the rest of the other inmates. He'd wait until they were directly outside the R.A S.C camp entrance close enough to slink away un-noticed and steal one of their jeeps. "A piece of cake," he'd boasted to an inmate, "I'll be halfway to Port Said by the time they realize I've gone."

But in spite of Private Crowe's meticulously detailed planning, he never did make it back home to Old Blighty after all. Not even close. He only got as far as Great Bitter Lake when he ran out of petrol and was picked up by the Red Caps (military police) who were more than happy to give him a free ride back to 50 MCE.

To make matters worse, private Crowe was not only charged with desertion and put behind bars for a lengthy time, but had his two-a-day cigarette ration taken away from him for a whole month, just as the Colonel had promised.

*****

One of the worst offenders for 'putting it on' was a scrawny little rabble-rouser from Glasgow. According to him, he'd suffered every disease, every affliction and every germ known to man. Hardly a day went by without him complaining about something, which in most cases was usually before dawn or just after midnight.

Brian made a point of warning me about Private Mitchell, telling me to be very wary of him. Always make sure he's been handcuffed before they bring him into the M.I. Room, he said, he can't be trusted. I asked one of the prison guards if he knew what Mitchell had done to deserve his six month stay in 50 M.C.E. "Sleeping on guard duty," he said, "he was found stretched out on a table inside the cookhouse, his loaded rifle leaning against the wall for all to see."

My first encounter with Private Mitchell happened one early morning when I was fast asleep in my bed. I felt someone touch my foot.

"WHO THE HELL'S THAT?"

It was pitch black. I couldn't see a damn thing in front of me, just two silhouetted figures standing at the foot of my bed.

"It's sergeant Moorcroft and one of the inmates, corporal," a voice said.

I switch on the flashlight and there's the little squirt with his hand over his mouth moaning and groaning. The same person that only a week ago had everyone in the camp (including me) searching all over the bloody desert for him, and at three o'clock in the morning no less. He'd grabbed the mattress off his bed and slung it over the barbed wire fencing making everyone believe he'd used it as an escape route, when all the time he was hiding in his tent wrapped up inside the tent wall. What a weird sense of humor is that, for God's sake?

"He's got toothache corporal," the Sergeant says, "he's in agony with it, says it's been keeping him awake most of the night."

"I hope this isn't one of your crazy pranks," I tell him, "because if it is, you're for the high jump mister, I promise you that!"

"It's not a prank," he says, taking his hand away from his mouth, "it's been giving me jip all night."

"Which one is it then? Open your mouth and let me see."

He sticks his finger inside his mouth and pulls out a brown tobacco stained pallet with three false teeth attached, one at the front and two at the back.

"Ish dish one," he mumbles, offering me his pallet, "dish one in the front, ish killing me."

Then there was Joe, the stocky bearded thirty year old college graduate from Devon. I can't remember what he'd done to warrant a three month stay at 50 MCE, but because of good behavior, he was given the freedom of the camp between the hours of ten in the morning until three in the afternoon.

One day, during one of our conversations, Joe tells me about his interest in hypnotism, how he'd learned the art of putting people under a 'spell'.

"Would you like me to show you how it's done?" He asked.

"No thanks," I said, "Not me, I don't want to be put under. And anyway I don't think I'm the right type."

"How do you know?"

"Because I'm too scared, it's as simple as that."

"Well, it doesn't work on everyone," he said, "Depends mostly on their personality. But I'll show you if you find someone who'll do it."

The days around camp dragged so we were always up for any distraction that might help pass the time. I open the door and look out across the camp square hoping I might see a suitable candidate.

"I think it could work on him," I said, pointing a finger in the direction of the cookhouse.

"Do you mean him standing outside the cookhouse smoking a cigarette?" Joe asked.

"Yeah, Robbie Allen, he'll be a perfect candidate I'm sure. Robbie's in a trance most of the time anyway. I'll call him over? I'd really like to see how it's done."

"Ok" Joe says, "Get him over here."

As it turns out, Robbie's excited about the whole idea. He doesn't seem to mind one bit about going under, just as long it doesn't take too long. Rather than being concerned about the hypnosis, his biggest concern seems to be getting back on time. Apparently Lance corporal Danny Richards only allows him ten minutes for a smoke, and not one minute longer.

> "Sit down in this chair Robbie," Joe says, "And cast your eyes on this tiny spot I've marked on the tent pole here."

Robbie sits himself down in the chair that Joe has placed close to the central tent pole.

> "Don't move your eyes off it," Joe says, "keep them firmly fixed on that little spot and listen carefully to what I tell you."

Robbie leans back in the chair nice and relaxed.

> "That's right Robbie, just sit back and relax and listen to my voice."

Within a very short space of time, Joe's got Robbie out cold; dead to the world. I was truly amazed how quickly it was done. And what happened next was even more amazing. Joe has Robbie stretched out across two chairs approximately four or five feet apart; the back of his head resting on one chair and his feet on the other, nothing in between to support the rest of his body.

> "I'm going to press down on your stomach now Robbie," Joe says, "but don't worry, your body's rigid, unbendable, it's as stiff as a board."

Joe presses firmly on Robbie's stomach with both his hands; Robbie doesn't even flinch. A minute or so later, when Robbie is still flat out across the two chairs, the door flies open and in charges lance corporal Danny Richards in a terrible temper.

“Is Robbie Allen in here?” he yells, “Because if he is, I’ll kill the skiving little.......What the f %&@#”.

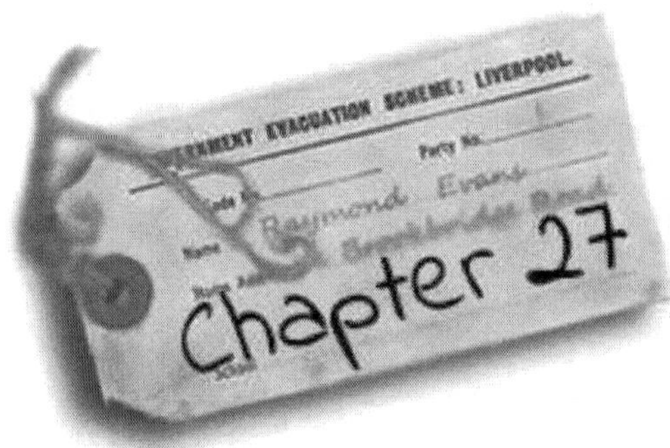

A Letter From Mum

Dateline: July, 1953.

Dear Raymond,

I'm very concerned, your letters are getting shorter and shorter and more infrequent. You used to write every couple of weeks, now it's once every two months, if I'm lucky. Just send me some news about yourself to let me know if you are alright.

Well, now that I've got that off my chest, I want to ask you something. Do you remember me telling you about the famous spiritualist from Liverpool, May Ross who I was planning to see? I mentioned it in my last letter a few weeks ago. Well, Elsie, Muriel and I finally managed to get an appointment with her just last week. I took your leather gloves with me in the hope she could tell me something about you, how you were keeping and so on. What an amazing person that lady is. After only a few seconds holding your gloves in her hands, she began complaining how hot she felt and asked if the owner of the gloves was in a hot climate somewhere? I told her you were in the army in Egypt.

She went on to tell me about that road accident you were involved in when you worked for Hanson's Dairies. That really surprised me considering no one had mentioned it so there's no way she could have known. She also asked me if I knew of a tall dark haired man with the initials T.M. a man with an artificial arm who had something to do with the accident. When I told her I didn't know anyone with those initials, she asked me who the petite young lady with dark brown hair is. I thought she meant Edith, but she said the person she was talking about wasn't related to anyone in the family and that she has the initial L in her name? You're not going out with some foreign lady over there are you, Raymond? I hope not.

By the way, I've sent you the food parcel you were asking about, so don't forget to write and let me know if it's arrived safely, remember, the last parcel went missing.

Love, Mum xx

The road accident my mother mentioned in her letter had happened not long after I started working for Hanson Dairies, shortly before starting my National Service in the army.

It was a bitterly cold and icy morning in (I'm guessing) March or April I think it was. The traffic on Queens Drive, the busy dual carriageway we were driving along had come to a complete stand-still due to a multiple crash close to the traffic lights. The road surface from one end of Queens Drive to the other was like an ice rink.

There were three of us in the cab that day, Jimmy Lutas, the driver, Pete Caddick (who would later marry my sister Muriel) and yours truly who was squashed up in the middle. We were about two hundred yards from the traffic lights, going about ten miles an hour in a low gear, when the lorry began gathering speed, and sliding out of control from one side of the road to the other. Jimmy somehow managed to change to an even lower gear, in an attempt to get more control over the vehicle, but it didn't help, the lorry just kept gathering speed heading ever closer to the abandoned vehicles piled up at the traffic lights. We were about fifty yards or so from the traffic lights, when I saw Pete's hand move towards the door handle getting ready to jump out. Seconds later the vehicle mounted the central median and turned over on its side, the driver's door facing up toward the sky. We had to climb up and squeeze through the window to get out. It was a terrifying few minutes that never fails to return whenever I'm driving in icy conditions.

Dear Mum,

The food parcel arrived yesterday morning all intact, thanks very much. I've really been looking forward to it, especially the tin of corned beef and the bar of Cadbury's fruit and nut chocolate.

I'm sorry I've not been writing as much as I used to, but there's not a lot I can tell you that I've not already mentioned before. Every day is the same in this place, nothing to do except to count the days until I will be leaving to come home. We're going through one of those periods when we're not allowed out of the camp, it's like being in jail. But please do not assume your letters are not worth receiving, because I really do look forward to them.

Regarding that spiritualist May Ross, she's absolutely right about one of the people she mentioned, the one with the initials T.M. I couldn't think of anyone right away until the other night just before dropping off to sleep. It came to me right out of the blue. She must've been talking about Ted Mosedale, one of the foremen at Hanson's Dairies who does, by the way, have an artificial arm.

I don't understand. It's so weird. How would she know all that? I've no idea who the other person is she's talking about, the one with the initial L in her name. Oh, and I'm not going out with anyone over here by the way, so you don't have to worry about that.

Love, Ray xx

Army As A Career

Colonel Bellamy still insists in trying to talk me into signing-on for another three years. Can you imagine that, three more years in this Godforsaken place? You MUST be joking colonel. What's wrong with you man? When are you going to realize I've no intentions of signing on, ever?

Don't get me wrong, I've nothing against army life, no complaints about doing my national service; everyone has to do their bit. It's just being locked up in this place twenty four hours a day, that's the problem. It's enough to drive a person crazy.

It's hot by day and cold at night

There's not a blasted thing that's right

I'm lost for words, can say no more

My mind is numb, my heart is sore

This place is desolate without a doubt

Roll on De-Mob and let's get out!

*****

The last time I was allowed outside of the camp gates was six weeks ago when I had to escort one of the inmates to hospital after getting injured in a fight. How nice it was to get away from the prison-like surroundings of 50 MCE for a few hours. Even the drive through the rat infested malarial villages was something of a novelty. Villages so old, you could easily assume they were built around the time King Tut was on his throne.

On the way to the hospital I asked Private Hobson, (a thin, dim-witted, frail looking guy who sat quietly gazing out of the window) what had started the fight that led to his arm getting broken.

"Well, I refused to split my cigarette ration with him," he said, "We only get two a day you know, that's all."

"Yes I know, but how did he come to actually break your arm?"

"I was trying to protect my head from the pick-axe handle he was hitting me with."

"Who's this **he** you keep going on about? What's his name?"

"I'm not tellin' you that!"

"Why?"

"Why? Because he'll do it again, that's why. He's mental."

His arm was set in a plaster cast at the hospital. On our way back to the camp the driver asks if it's ok, if he drives over to one of the shops at Great Bitter Lake so he can buy a souvenir for his mother.

"Okay, but you've only got five minutes to find something," I told him.

"I know exactly what I want, he said, "a table cloth. She likes those fancy woven ones they make over here."

"Well as long as you know which shop it is that sells them, because I'm not hanging around there for long, it's far too dangerous."

"Harrods," he said, pointing a finger to a small strip of makeshift shops about three hundred yards away. "That's who sells them."

"Harrods? I said. "Are you serious? This better not be one of your jokes because if it is, you can forget about your mother's tablecloth."

"I'm not joking, he said, "I thought you knew about these shops."

All the typical British high street names were represented. There was a shoe shop to the left of Harrods trading under the name of Timpsons. Next door to that, a camera shop trading as Famous Kodak Cameras. This was THE major "dirt track" (it would be misleading to call it a road) between several camps and garrisons around and in between Fayid and Ismalia. Obviously the enterprising owners of these ramshackle huts, masquerading as shops, thought they'd have a better chance of catching the attention of the many military personnel by using the familiar names over their stores.

Shops with familiar British names close to the Moascar and Fayid camps.(Img. SuezCanalZone.com)

The driver pulled up and raced into Harrods while I stayed in the vehicle handcuffed to the inmate.

"S'pose these people fink by using English names above their shops they'll sell a lot more of their goods to the British soldiers," the inmate observed.

"Yes, that seems to be the idea. Are there anymore shops around here with English names?"

"Yes," he said, "there's one at the end of this block called Selfridges. They sell leather photo albums, hand-bags, wallets, belts and stuff like that."

It was just then I heard a lot of commotion coming from inside the Harrods shop. I jumped out of the Jeep dragging the inmate behind me.

"What the hell's going on," I shouted, as I entered the shop, "what's all the shouting about?"

"That little sod was about to throw a bottle of liquid shoe polish over me," the driver said, pointing his finger at the little boy behind the counter.

"All because I wouldn't pay his tight fisted Dad over there the price he's asking for this tablecloth - robbing bastard."

"He bastard," the shop keeper says, tugging at my sleeve. "Every time he come in shop he want everything too cheap. He is robbing bastard, Corporal, not me."

"Stick your bloody tablecloth," the driver says, "that's the last time I'll come in here."

The foul language and name calling coming out of the driver's mouth incites even more trouble. And in no time at all, an angry mob of fist waving shopkeepers appear from what seems like nowhere, trying to prevent us from getting to the Jeep. One of them was even waving a very large machete type knife above his head shouting, "BRITISH TOMMY BASTARDS! BRITISH TOMMY BASTARDS!"

Thankfully, just as I'm thinking there's a good possibility I'll never see England ever again, a white MP's truck screeches up and four Red-Caps jump out. Their timing couldn't have been better if they were the Cavalry in a John Wayne movie!

About a week later I'm sitting at my desk writing the daily report when I hear an ambulance come screaming through the camp gates. A few minutes later I see Private Hobson being carried out on a stretcher, the same young lad I'd escorted to the hospital. His head had been bashed in by the same person who broke his arm a couple of weeks earlier; and all because he refused to split his cigarette ration with him. He was immediately flown back to England for an emergency operation on his badly fractured skull. The poor lad died in hospital a few days later. His attacker was flown back to England to stand trial for murder.

Anyway getting back to the story, evenings were by far the worst part of the day. There was nothing much else to do except to either lounge on my bed and escape into a book, or stroll over to the NAFFI (Navy, Army and Air Force Institute) tent for a game of darts and bottle of Stella beer. How exciting is that, I wanted to ask the Colonel the next time he asked me to sign on? It's all right for you Colonel, living down the road in that nice posh house of yours, being waited on twenty four hours a day. And where's this tented cinema you keep promising us? The Astra Cinema in town has been out of bounds for over three months now, another one of your empty promises is it, Colonel?

Most every night I stand and stare

Across the desert, crude and bare

Sometimes I sit beneath the moon

And dream of Blighty in mid-June

Of times I had when I was there

With this place I cannot compare

This camp is desolate without a doubt

Roll on de-mob, and let's get out!

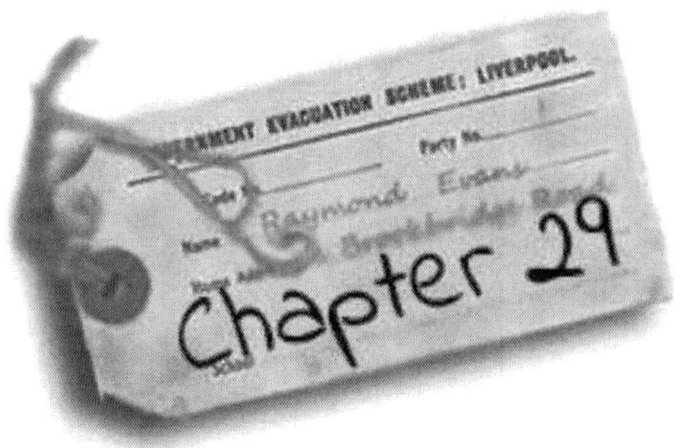

De-Mob Delight

It was sometime during the latter part of August, a few weeks before my long awaited discharge from the Army. I was sitting alone enjoying the coolness of the camp church, playing a one finger rendition of 'Amazing Grace' on the organ when someone crept up from behind and tapped me on the shoulder. I was staggered to see it was an old school pal of mine, Bobby Jones. He'd driven over 20 miles just to come to see me, and I didn't even know he was in the army, never mind in Egypt.

Bobby was a corporal in the R.A.S.C. (Royal Army Service Corps). He'd been given the job of driving the camp colonel around. I kept looking at the bloke standing next to him, wondering where I'd seen him before. It took me a minute or so before I realized who he was.

"It's not Norman is it?" I said, "Not that skinny fella from Crosby, the one I met on the train in Lime Street Station all that time ago?"

Norman Pickles smiled broadly as he shook my hand. It was a strong firm handshake this time, so different from the limp wimpy handshake he'd given me when we first met on the train in Lime Street station.

"Wow! I can't believe how you've changed Norman,"

"For the better I hope" was his reply.

"Yes," I said, "definitely for the better. You've put on a bit of weight since I last saw you and you've grown a moustache; my God your parents won't recognize you when you get home. You look so different from when we first met on the train that day a couple of years ago!"

"Counting the days are you?" he asked, "Or are you thinking of signing on for another three?"

"Oh sure," I said, "When pigs fly."

"I met up with Norman a few months ago when he was posted to our camp," Bobby said, "and believe it or not, **he is** thinking of signing on - for another **five**."

"Is that true Norman or his he joking?"

"No, he's not joking," he said, "I really like the army life. I've found it suits me."

"I can't believe what I'm hearing" I said, "You're the last person in the world I'd have expected to sign on. I mean, you hated the army so much a few of us had to talk you out of doing a runner, do you remember that, Norman?"

"Yes I do," he said, "but people **can** change, you know. I really do like being in the army now. I think it's a great life, as long as they don't send me back here again, that's the only concern I have."

I met up with Bobby the following year shortly after his demobilization. He told me that Norman had in fact changed his mind about signing on for another five.

"It doesn't surprise me," I said, "Norman just wasn't the type."

"You think so?" Bobby said.

"Yes, I knew he wouldn't sign on."

"Well your wrong there, Ray, because he did sign on – not for another five, but FOR ANOTHER TEN!"

*****

The remaining few months of my National Service, were spent planning what I intended to do with my life once I received my demobilization papers. Returning to my old job, working for Hanson's would be my first move. That would give me time to look for something better. Under government law, because they were my last employer prior to going in the army, I knew they were duty-bound to take me back on. Nonetheless, I had no intentions of staying there for any length of time. I had no desire in driving a milk lorry for the rest of my life. Nor did I want to be working in some factory six days a week, struggling from one wage packet to the next. I did however have aspirations of starting up a business of some sort; of owning my home rather than renting as my parents had to all of their lives.

Looking back, I think my dreams and desires were mostly born out of my wartime experiences as an evacuee. Because I'd spent six years living in other people's homes feeling like a beggar, I wanted to be sure I'd never have to rely on other people's charity ever again.

I truly believed and still do, that nothing is impossible as long as you're willing to work hard, and try new things. Just like my father had told me, many times over. I fully intended to do anything, and everything, to ensure that my life going forward - would be defined by me, and on my own terms, rather than other peoples. I just didn't know quite how or what I was going to do to make that happen, but I was "working" on it!

Land of sorrow, filth and shame

I've seen you once but never again

I leave you now with no regret

But sights I've seen I'll not forget

Natives Heaven, white man's Hell

This hot dusty land

I fare thee well

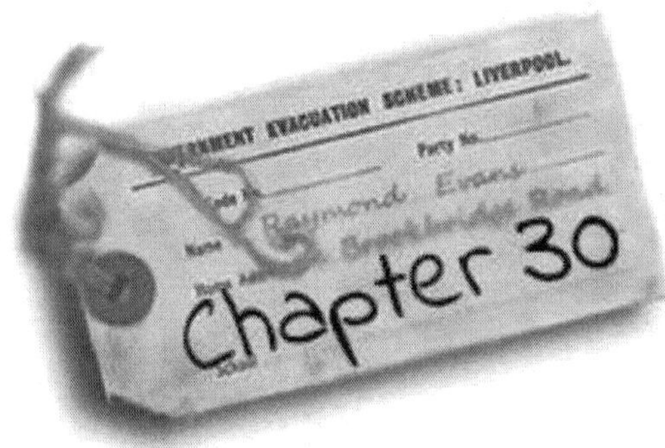

Lime St to East Lanc's Labyrinth

Dateline: 30th September, 1953.

Stepping off the train is like stepping back into a recurring bad dream. Even though I'm twenty years of age, Lime Street Station still holds (for me anyway) the most miserable associations from the past. It's the place where I was separated from my family, when I became an evacuee at the start of the war in 1939 - a place that represents separation, anxiety and loneliness, even though I'm returning home.

"Where to lad?" asks the taxi driver in his thick Liverpool accent.

"Cubert Road please, it's on the new Gillmoss estate."

He eyes me cautiously.

"Do yer mean one of those new 'ousing estates out by the East Lancashire Road, is that where yer goin?"

"Yes, I think that's where it is, close to the English Electric factory, or so I've been told."

"Well with that tan and all the kit you're carryin' yer look like you're comin' ome from **somewhere** lad. So how cum you only think it's close to the English Electric factory?"

"Because I'm not sure exactly where it is, that's why. My family moved while I was over in Egypt doing my national service. I've never been there before."

A little further on:

"What road did yer say it was again?"

"Cubert Road. There's a sign for the Gillmoss Estate just opposite the English Electric factory, that's all you need to look for."

The English Electric factory that had once produced ammunition for the war effort , was now (after being re-tooled) producing consumer goods, that would fuel what would become known in retrospect as the 'past war boom.'

In their infinite wisdom, local government officials decided they could solve two issues, housing and workforce relocation, with one stone. So they planned and built a massive housing estate out at Gill Moss to provide housing for the many displaced families with proximity to work at GE or the new ICI plant that was just a little further up the East Lanc's Road. The problem was; it was so far removed from public transport, no one, not even the people who lived there, could find their way around the labyrinth of streets and houses that all looked exactly the same, interspersed by the occasional three story block of flats.

There's a well-known saying: 'The definition of insanity is repeating the same behavior and expecting a different result.' Yet the very same government bodies did exactly that, over and over again in the following decades when they built places like Skelmersdale, Kirby, and as late as the 70's, Runcorn, a place where famous Liverpool comedian John Bishop once described as a "Social experiment". As someone who was born in Liverpool, whose family was relocated to Runcorn - he hilariously describes how the town planners decided in their infinite wisdom that "for working-class Scouser's to be happy, each council estate needed a shop, a chippy and a pub!"

Back to the story:

> "I 'ope yer know where yer goin' mate, cos I 'aven't seen any signs pointin to Gillmoss, not yet anyway. It's a bloody nightmare drivin' round those bloody new 'ousing estates I don't mind tellin' yer. I'm not lookin' forward to it one little bit. All those bloody streets look alike to me."

We've travelled a few more miles when the silence is broken with more unsavory comments.

> "Where the 'ell are we now? We've been goin' along this same road for God's knows 'ow long an' I still 'aven't

seen one bloody sign for Gilmoss. Are yer **sure** you've got the right directions?"

It's around this time that he begins to slow down, that I get the feeling he's about to change his mind and refuse to continue on the journey.

"Please, can you just go a little further; the rain's coming down sideways out there?"

"Sorry son, I've come far enough, I'm turnin' round."

"You mean you're going to drop me off here, in the middle of nowhere? Well thanks a lot."

As luck would have it, the Gillmoss sign was little more than a quarter of a mile further on, directly opposite the English Electric Factory, just like my mother had mentioned in her letter. The trouble was, because she hadn't bothered to include precise directions to Cubert Road, I didn't have a clue which direction I should take once I'd reached the bottom of Gillmoss Lane. I found myself in the middle of a vast housing estate getting drenched to the skin with no idea whether Cubert Road was around the next corner or three miles away.

The heavy rain was keeping people indoors so there was no one around to ask for directions. My only other option was to knock on someone's door and ask for their help.

"Sorry to bother you, but I'm trying to find Cubert Road, any idea?"

"Can't help you there laddy, we're strangers around these parts. We only moved in a few weeks ago, all the way from Scotland."

"Yes, I can tell from your accent."

"Why don't you try the Fire Station, they're bound to have a map of the estate? That's what I'd do if I were you."

"Oh, now that's a great idea, where **is** the Fire Station?"

"Dunno' son, like I just said; we've only been here a few weeks."

"What about a Police Station then?"

"Nope, don't have one yet either, but there are rumors they're going to build one just down the road from here."

"Well thanks anyway," I tell him, trying to make sense of what he's just told me. "I'll try further down the road."

I'm beginning to wonder if I'll ever find Cubert Road when I hear the feint sound of a vehicle approaching from behind. I step off the pavement to flag him down.

"Sorry to stop you, I'm looking for Cubert Road, would you happen to know where it is?"

"I should do. I live there" says the driver.

"Well, thank God for that, can you direct me?"

"I'll do better than that, I'll take you there… jump in lad."

"Thanks a lot. It's number thirty four."

"Yes, I know. You must be Mrs. Evans's son?"

"Yes, how did you know?"

"She told me you were due home from the army, we live practically opposite."

The kindly neighbor weaves his way through the streets and drops me off in front of the latest Evans family residence. I thank him, grab my kitbag lug it to the front door and ring the bell. Albert opens the door, clearly not expecting me!

"Good God, is that you Ray?" he says as he wraps me in a big bear hug.

"Yes Al, it's me."

"How are you? Blimey, you are tanned! I couldn't see you properly in the dark. Here, let me help you with your kit bag."

"Who is it Albert?" My mother shouts from the lounge. "Was that someone at the door?"

"It's our Raymond."

"Raymond did you say?"

"Yes, he's back home from Egypt."

My mother comes rushing into the hall followed by Muriel, Dorothy, Edith, Stanley and the youngest of the family, David who's now twelve.

"I wasn't expecting you until tomorrow," my mother says, "I must have got the days mixed up. How did you manage to find the house?"

"The man opposite gave me a lift, Mr. Windsor, if he hadn't come along I'd probably still be out there walking around in circles."

"Oh my gosh, what a welcome home for you! Well, take those wet things off while I put the kettle on and make you a nice cup of tea. Do you want something to eat, you looked starved."

"When are you going back?" asks Dorothy. "How long are you home for?"

"Going back? How long am I home for? Are you kidding me? I'm home for good. I've done my time, two years national service is more than enough for me thank you very much, I'm done!"

"You mean you've been away for **two whole** years already," Edith says. "Seems like only six months since you walked out of here on your way to the station. Can't believe it," she says, shaking her head. "No I can't, either," Dorothy says, "it's absolutely flown over, no doubt about that!"

The following couple of weeks were spent mostly relaxing and enjoying being at home, enjoying my mother's cooking and getting used to being back home with my brothers and sisters around. Dad on the other hand, was still on the high seas, not due home for another couple of months.

After allowing myself a couple of weeks to settle back into home life, it was back to Hanson's Dairies, my last job prior to my two year stint in the army. It was to be a short term move where I would remain just long enough to take advantage of the company's program to help employees learn to drive and obtain a driving license. This way I could learn to drive on the job using the company's vehicles, and save myself the prohibitive cost of paying for driving lessons. The only problem, there were more than a few other employees with the same idea! This meant having to wait another full year before they would allow my 'L' plates (Learner Driver) to be fixed to the back of a company vehicle. Although I hated the job and was impatient to move on, I decided to stick it out until I was able to take my driving test which I passed on my first attempt.

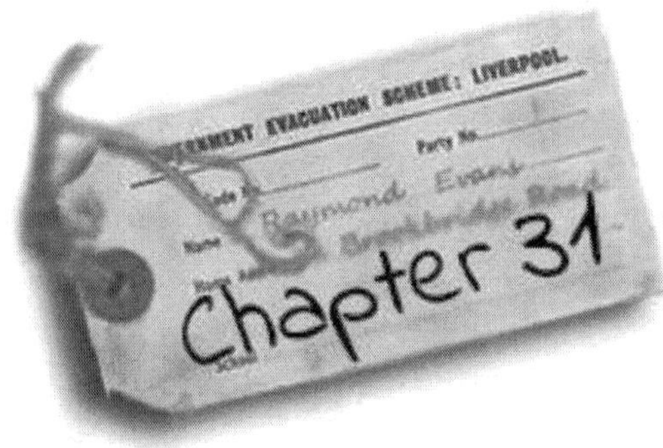

Dancing To A Date

Dateline: November, 1953.

I was thumbing through the paper one Sunday evening when I came across a tiny advertisement tucked away in the entertainment section.

'Dancing is not only an enjoyable art form, but a leisure interest that will help you make new friends.'

I zeroed in...

ARTHUR EDWARD'S SCHOOL of DANCING

Belmont Road, Liverpool

EVENINGS, 7.30 - 10.30. Admission... 1/6d

I sat for a moment staring down at the advert seeing myself stumbling around the dance floor bumping into everyone.

"Do you fancy coming with me?" I asked Albert, passing him the newspaper.

"Learn to dance? Nah, not me."

"What about you Stan? Will you come with me? I'll pay; it's only one and six."

"When?"

"Monday"

"Nah, don't fancy learning to dance."

"Go on your own," my mother says, "I'm sure there'll be plenty of other beginners there besides you."

Although I felt nervous about going on my own, looking back, I was glad I did because had I not plucked up the courage, I wouldn't have met up with Lilian; the slim pretty seventeen year old whom I instantly fell for. The wonderful person I've been married to for the past fifty seven years. And incredible as it may seem, the same young lady the spiritualist May Ross had mentioned to my mother all that time ago, the young lady with the dark brown hair and the initial 'L' in her name.

I'm greeted at the door by Arthur Edwards, a short, slim middle aged man wearing a smart double-breasted suit and a shiny pair of black patent leather shoes.

"The dance room is down the hall on your right," he says, as I hand him my one shilling and sixpence entrance fee, "the door opposite the cloak room. Take a seat, the others will be arriving shortly."

The weather was particularly bad with heavy rain and unusually strong winds that night, so only six people turned up - Audrey, Arthur Edward's assistant, followed by three pretty teenage girls and two well-dressed young men.

Arthur Edwards plugs in the record player, places a record on the turn-table and two couples get up to dance. This makes me even more nervous sitting in the corner watching them glide around the floor with the artistry of Fred Astaire and Ginger Rogers. Just as they finished dancing and had returned to their seats, Audrey, a tall slim twenty year old comes over and sits down beside me.

"You look a little nervous."

"Yes, because it looks like I'm the only first-timer here."

She smiles and assures me that none of the others could dance a step when they first started.

"Come with me," she says, taking hold of my arm, "I want to introduce you to someone."

I follow her to the far end of the room where three young girls are busy chatting among themselves.

"This is Lilian," she says, "one of our Monday night regulars. When the music starts, she's going to show you the basic steps of the waltz. She's very good, just try and be a little gentle with her. Try to avoid stepping on those tiny little toes of hers."

"The Waltz is quite simple," Lilian says, as we make our way to the center of the dance floor.

"There are only three steps to it. Lead with the left foot by putting it straight out in front of you, just like this, then bring the right foot forward and to the side before bringing the left foot across to the right. Just three steps, that's all there is to it, one-two- three, one-two-three, and so on. Are you okay with that before I ask Audrey to start the music?"

"Erm, what was it again? Right foot first or left foot?"

"No, no, left foot first then the right foot. Watch me again, watch how I do it."

"Okay, I think I've got it now."

"Good," she says, as she nods to Audrey for the music to start.

"No, no, you're doing it again; you're starting with your right foot when you should be starting with your left foot."

"Sorry, can we start again?"

"Yes, ok. Just wait for the beat - I'll tell you when."

"Sorry, I'm a little nervous."

What a night it turned out to be. It would've been far less embarrassing had there been at least one other 'first-timer' on the floor besides me; someone who did not know his left foot from his right - who moved around the room with all the grace and composure of the proverbial bull in a china shop.

However, as I've already mentioned, meeting up with Lilian that evening made it all worthwhile. She'd caught my attention the moment I entered the room. In fact I became so infatuated with her during the evening, I was determined (before the night was over) to pluck up the courage and ask if she would let me take her home. The trouble was, I wasn't sure if she'd come to the dance school on her own or with one of the two boys that were there; maybe the one who kept getting her up to dance all evening. The only way to find out was to wait in the doorway when everyone was leaving

So there I was, sheltering from the rain at the top of the steps when suddenly she came flying past holding an umbrella above her head shouting good night to everyone. I hadn't noticed him standing by his car holding the door for her to get in; the same chap who'd kept getting her up to dance most of the evening.

I lay in bed that night thinking about her, seeing her pretty face in my mind's eye smiling back at me. I'd taken a serious fancy to her - I had to see her again.

*****

all I want is a peaceful world and a pork pie!

Dateline: 22nd May, 1954.

"It's been six months since I last saw her," I tell my sister, Muriel, "I know it sounds a bit silly, but I can't stop thinking about her."

"Are you sure he wasn't just giving her a lift home out of the rain. He might not be her boyfriend after all, have you not thought about that?"

"No, I haven't, well, not until recently. That's why I was thinking of going back on Monday to find out if she **is** going out with him."

"Why Monday?"

"Because that's her usual night for going."

"Then that's what you should do, that's the only way you're going to find out, isn't it?"

"Yes I know, but...

"But what?"

"Well, would you mind teaching me to do the waltz? I'd feel a lot more confident going back knowing I can at least do one dance without making a fool of myself."

"Ah, so that's why we've been having this conversation, you crafty little thing. I was wondering why you were giving away all your little secrets."

“You're not going to tell the others about this conversation we’re having, are you?”

“The others?”

“Yes. Franky, Albert and Stanley! Can we **please** keep this to ourselves; you know what they’re like for taking the mickey.”

“Don’t worry, I won't tell them.” she promised.

“Thanks. By the way, Mum said we could use the parlor as long as we're careful not to knock anything over.

“So you've thought of everything, haven't you? I just hope for your sake this girl you like is still going to that dance school; six months is a long time."

"Yes, so do I, I keep thinking she may have stopped going altogether. I hope I'm wrong."

"Wait a minute; you **did** say you wanted to learn the waltz, right?"

"Yes; why?"

"Because I don't think we've got a waltz record - that's why."

“We have. I bought one yesterday on my way home from work.”

“You did?"

"Yes."

"All part of this little plan of yours, no doubt? Which one did you get?"

"The Tennessee Waltz; they played it that night at the dance school

As things turned out, much to my delight, she **was** there that night. She was in the middle of a crowded dance floor dancing the quick-step when I walked in. But it wasn't until she was back in her seat that I was able to get a proper look at her. That's when she saw me staring at her, when she gave me the same warm smile that had remained locked in my memory throughout the previous six months. I got her up to dance three or four times during the evening; each time making sure it was a waltz that they were playing.

That night marked the beginning of a two and a half year courtship that ultimately led to our marriage on September 1, 1956.

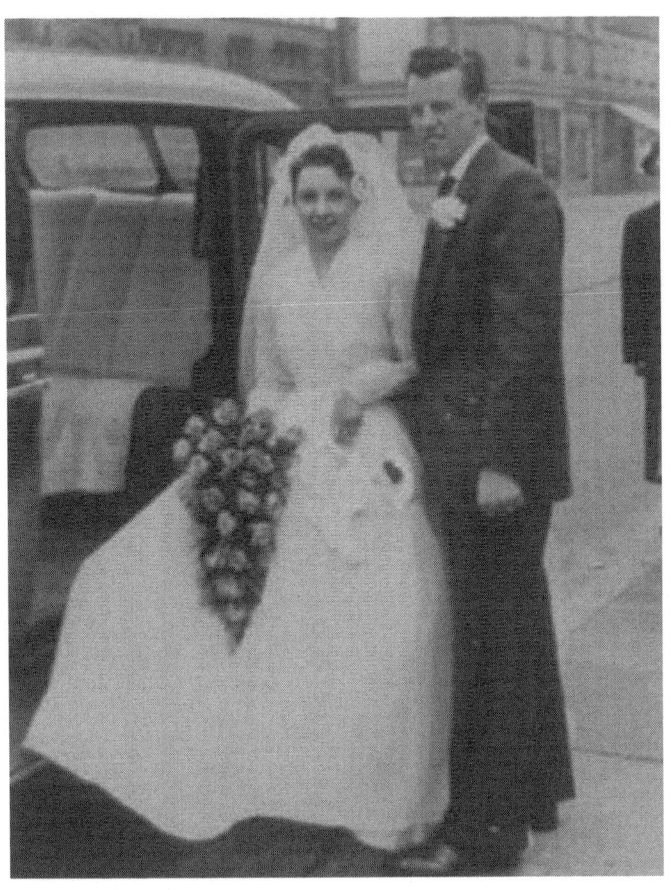

Lilian and I on our wedding day.

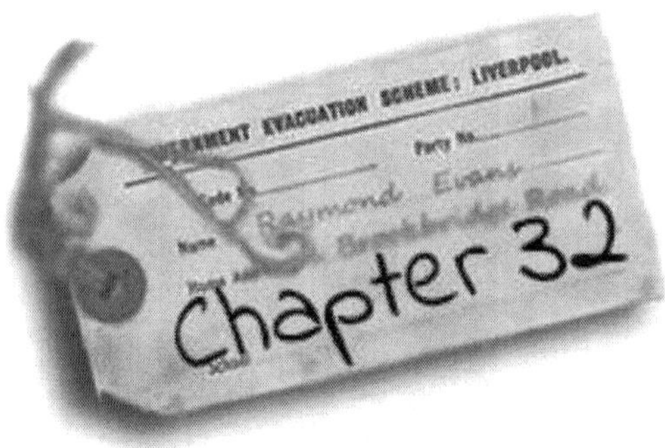

Lino Paint & Pork Pies

Our first home was a two bedroom top floor flat in Botanic Road - about three maybe four miles from the city centre. Property owner, Robert J Jones; (the father of long standing friend, Bobby Jones) the man who was the owner of the flat, gave us an excellent deal by reducing the rent to nearly half.

It didn't take long for us to get it cleaned up and cozy looking before moving in. My mother; an expert at hanging wallpaper, offered to paper the lounge ceiling, a job I would not even **think** of tackling. The rest of the flat which consisted of a tiny kitchen, two bedrooms and a bathroom, I decorated myself on my days off.

One evening as we were getting ready to leave the flat, Lilian looked down at the floor in the hallway and said:

> "I've just had a thought, what about painting the hall floor a different colour?"

"Paint the hall floor? Why would you want to do that? I asked. "That's expensive in-laid linoleum, it's practically new?"

“I know," she said, "but it doesn’t suit the new colour scheme."

"When did you think of this?"

"Just now, as I was putting my coat on to leave."

"But paint will wear off in no time, surely.”

“Lino paint,” she said, “it's not like ordinary paint.”

“Lino paint?”

“Yes. It’s a brand new product that’s just come on the market. One of the girls in work told me about it just yesterday.”

"Okay, what colour would you like it painting?”

“French Navy; it’ll coordinate nicely with the wallpaper you’ve just put up.”

“Right, I’ll do it next Thursday morning on my day off. Where do I get this Lino paint from?"

"From the same shop we bought the wallpaper,” she said, “that one around the corner from the flat, next door to Watsons the Bakers."

"Watson's the Bakers? Isn't that where you get the pork pies from?"

"Yes" she said.

*****

It's nine thirty when I arrive at the flat the following Thursday morning. I padlock my bike to the railings, take out the can of Lino paint and two pork pies from inside the carrier bag and make my way up the steps to the front door.

Mrs. Caldicot, a white-haired seventy year old retired school teacher (who loves to talk for long periods of time) comes out of her flat at the exact moment I step into the hallway.

"Mmm, something smells nice," she says, pointing a finger at the brown paper bag I'm carrying, "been to the bakers I see."

"Yes, I've just treated myself to a couple of pork pies for when I've finished the painting. They've just come out of the oven. I couldn't resist the smell as I passed the bakery. So I'm rushing to get the painting finished before they go cold."

"Oh, and what might you be painting now?" she asks, in her ever-so-posh school mistress voice.

"The hall floor."

"But I thought you'd finished all the painting and decorating?"

"Almost, just the hall floor to do now - that's all."

"The hall floor, you're going to paint the hall floor?"

"Yes. Lilian doesn't like the colour of the linoleum that's down there; she doesn't think it suits the wallpaper. Anyway, I really have to go, my pies are getting cold. Bye for now."

"Just a minute," she shouts, as I start up the stairs. "Did you say Lino paint just then?"

"Yes, that's right, Lino paint."

"Never heard of it."

"It's new. It's just come on the market. Must go; bye!"

"Why don't you eat them now while they're still hot?"

"Sorry?"

"The pies; they'll go cold if you don't eat them now!"

"Oh, I'd rather get the painting taken care of first then I can relax and enjoy them. I'll pop them in the oven for a few minutes. I really must go, Mrs. Caldicot. See you!"

"In the oven, did you say?"

"Yes, in the oven. Bye!"

It doesn't seem to matter to her that I'm now half way along the second landing approaching the third flight of stairs, nor what ear piercing level she has to raise her voice in order for me to hear what she's saying - she still continues with her questions:

"Have the gas people been then? I thought they weren't due till next week to switch on your gas supply? That's what Lilian told me the other day?"

"You're right. I forgot about that. Anyway, it really doesn't matter. I'm a fast painter. They'll still be warm when I've finished the painting. Speak to you later!"

"Just a minute Ray, before you go. **HELLO!** Can you still hear me? I'll put them in my oven for you if you like. It's no bother. I don't mind, really. **HELLOOOO! CAN YOU HEAR ME UP THERE?"**

I feel guilty for ignoring her. The poor lady is on her own, she's got no one to talk to. I'm sorry missus, I say under my breath as I step inside the flat, but I do need to get on with the painting.

My pies are getting colder by the minute!

I throw off my coat, grab a small dinner plate off the kitchen shelf, and grab the tea-cozy out of the cupboard (to help preserve the heat for as long as possible) as I carefully slide my two pies inside the tea-cozy. Having taken care of all that; I then quickly slip into my decorating overalls and get busy painting the hall floor. And because it's only about fifteen feet long by three feet wide, I don't expect it'll take me too long to arrive at the other end. My stomach rumbles a little.

Now, of all the things I'm not very good at, failing to concentrate on the job at hand has to be the most outstanding.

No matter what the job may be, I never fail to go off into a little world of my own. When I got up off my hands and knees at the far end of the hall, was when I realized what I'd done.

Oh sh** a voice inside my head shouted. Look what you've done, you've gone and painted yourself into the bloody bedroom!

I picked up the can to check the directions, wondering how long does Lino paint take to dry? Could be one of those quick drying paints, I tell myself hopefully, it's quite possible. Please God, let it be quick drying paint...

ALLOW SEVEN TO EIGHT HOURS TO DRY

BEST LEFT OVERNIGHT.

Initially I think I've no option but to walk on it...

There's no way I'm hanging around here all day literally watching paint dry.

Then, just as I'm about to step into the hallway, my foot literally inches away from the wet paint, I get this sudden brainstorm. I step back and take off my shoes, hang them around my neck using the laces and stuff the socks inside my trouser pockets. I then stretch my arms out to the sides at shoulder height and step up onto the thick wooden molding that runs along the base of the wall on either side. I'm now able to maneuver myself along the hallway by pressing my hands against the walls allowing me to 'walk' along the 'skirting' board with just the edges of my bare feet. As difficult as it is to balance, I manage to "shuffle" my way down the length of the hall to the front door, open it and stumble out onto the landing.

And it was while I was sitting on the stairs putting my shoes and socks back on that I suddenly remembered about meeting up with Lilian. We had planned to meet at twelve o'clock outside her office in Bold Street in the city centre. Time was fast running out. It'd turned eleven thirty already. I'd just half an hour to get on my bike and search for a telephone box to let her know I wouldn't make it on time.

Now, before I go any further, you may be wondering why I'm not calling her on my cell phone. Well, this was the nineteen fifties don't forget. Things were so very different back then. Most people didn't even **have** a telephone in the house never mind a cell phone. The Black-Berry's and smartphones, so common today had never even been heard of, those were still the stuff of science fiction at that time. As were Palm Pilots, Lap tops, ear receivers, laser guided thing-a-me-jigs, iPods or iPads and pretty much everything else with an acronym for a name!

Anyway, back to the story:

"Hello, can I speak to Miss. Hewitt please, it is urgent.

"Hello."

"Hi, it's me, Ray."

"Is there something wrong, you sound out of breath?"

"No, there's nothing wrong. It's just that I won't be able to meet for lunch like we'd planned."

"Why not?"

"I'll explain later when I come to pick you up tonight. It's too long a story. Have to go. Love you. Bye."

"Love you too, bye."

*****

"Why weren't you able to meet me for lunch," Lilian asked. "What happened?"

"Because I was still in my decorating overalls."

"In your overalls?"

"Yes."

"I don't understand - where was your jacket?"

"In the lounge keeping my two pork pies company."

“Then why didn't you go in and get it?”

“I couldn't.”

“You couldn't?”

"No."

“Why?”

“Because it meant stepping on the wet p.........”

“Oh, now I see. Now I get it,” she said, trying her best to stop herself from laughing. “You painted yourself in, didn’t you? That’s what you were about to say just then?”

I bought this Ford Thames van (used) for £100.
Little did I know how much I would need a van
rather than a car very soon!

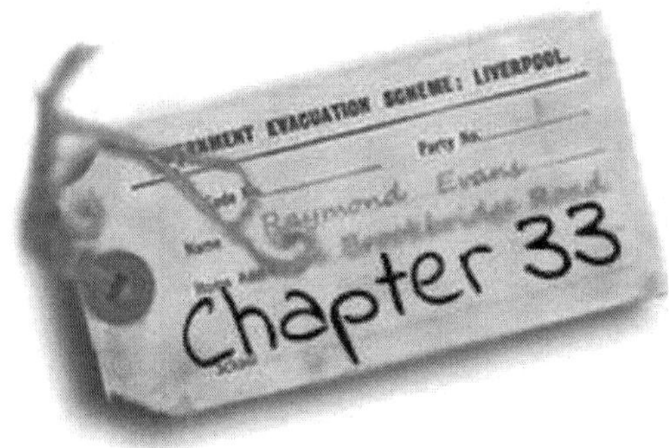

Barber Shop Brainwave

Dateline: November, 1956.

It's a Thursday morning and I'm in my local barber shop thumbing through an old magazine when I happen to come across the following article:

HOW TO START A BUSINESS ON A SHOESTRING

I'm about to turn the page for more details when the barber, a short stocky seventy year old who's been cutting hair and giving advice for close on fifty years, shouts next. He doesn't like his customers reading while he's cutting their hair so while he's not looking I tear out the page and stuff it in my jacket pocket.

I went straight into the bedroom when I got home and put the torn out article on my nightstand with the intention of reading it later that night before going to sleep. I wished I hadn't read the article because it kept me awake for quite a while. My brain was working overtime wondering if it were really possible for a person to start up a business with (as the article in the magazine had so clearly stated) little or no money.

I lay there for nearly an hour racking my brain until I eventually came to the conclusion it just wasn't worth losing more sleep over and slid the paper back onto the nightstand with the intention of maybe looking at it again tomorrow. However, that wasn't the end of it. I woke up at about two o'clock that morning (just three hours before my alarm would go off and I would need to get up for work) and in seconds my mind had returned to the article. I decided I'd get up, make myself a cup of tea and have another read.

The gist of the article was that you simply need to find a way to solve a problem common to most people. Once you can identify the problem, all you need to do is figure out a better solution and make it available to as many people as possible.

It was when I was lifting the heavy galvanized metal washing tub from the top of the stove to make room for the kettle that the idea suddenly came to me. I grabbed a notepad and pen, sat down at the kitchen table and began scratching out ideas. I became more and more excited as my idea began to take shape.

Before I take this story any further, I should explain the concept of "wash-day" and what that actually entailed for many women in England as recently as the late 1950's. Looking at it now, I'm struck by the fact that this was without doubt a tough and thankless task. A back breaking process that thousands of women repeated week in and week out; often from the moment they were old enough to complete the task, and often until they were either too old or too weak to do it any longer!

Wash days for my mother after the war (when all the family were back at home and living together) had to be spent in the old Dickensian type 'Communal Wash House' down the street. There was no way possible the little copper boiler in the corner of our kitchen could have coped with the huge amount of washing that accumulated each and every day. With the help of my two sisters she would collect the dirty washing, bundle it all up in one of the bed sheets like a gargantuan Christmas pudding, load it on to an old pram, and have one of us push it across the park to the Kensington Wash House. I hated it when she had to go to that place, watching her standing in ankle deep water scrubbing away at the mountain of clothes.

Britain's first wash house was influenced by Catherine 'Kitty' Wilkinson, and opened up in Liverpool way back in 1842. She had for years, opened up her own home to her poorer neighbors to wash their clothes, mostly those who didn't have running water in their homes, who only had access to a communal stand-pipe in the middle of the street. Kitty and her husband Tom were acknowledged by the authorities when they offered them the role of superintendents at Liverpool's first wash house in Upper Frederick Street – not that far from the city center.

Each person would be allocated a 'stall' or 'laundry area' that was fitted with a boiler, a large stone basin, a washboard, a hand wringer and a very large chunk of hard green soap – all at the cost of just nine pence (9d), the price that was charged when wash-houses opened in 1842.

It's hard to comprehend that that same old wash-house was still operating over a 100 years later, the place where my mother was able to get all her washing done in just one short day - the place that would light the embers of an idea that came to me early one morning in that little flat in Botanic Road.

*****

It was around four o 'clock when I heard Lilian moving around in the bedroom. I was stretched out on the couch with the note-pad on my knee scribbling away when she walked sleepily into the room rubbing her eyes.

"Why are you up so early? She asked, "What time is it?"

"Four o'clock, I'm sorry, did I wake you up?"

"It's okay, what are you doing?"

"How would you like a washing machine?"

"Sorry, I'm still half asleep, say that again."

"A washing machine, you know; one of those new machines that does the washing instead of having to use a dolly tub."

"Yes, of course I'd like a washing machine. I'd have bought one long ago if we'd had the money. It'd definitely make life a lot easier. But what makes you ask that now?"

"What if someone came round to the house each week and hired you one?"

"I'm not sure what you mean," she said, sipping her tea, "who hires out washing machines?"

"I don't know if they do, but never mind that for the moment, **would** you hire one if they did?"

"Well depending on how much they were charging, of course I would. It would save me a lot of time and work"

"How about if they charged you, say, three shillings for an hour?"

"Three shillings an hour, I'd definitely do it for that, why, who **is** doing it?"

"Nobody as far as I know; not yet, anyway."

The washing machines I'm talking about here were not the size or weight of present day machines, not by a long chalk. If they were I'd have needed the strength of Charles Atlas to lug them around, especially up and down three flights of stairs to the flats!

“So **you’re** thinking of doing this, is that what you’re trying to tell me?”

“Well yes. I really believe it’ll work.”

“What made you come up with that idea?”

“I read something yesterday in a magazine about starting up a business and it’s been on my mind ever since. Actually, I woke up at two this morning and immediately started thinking about it again. So I got up and made a cup of tea. And I’m glad I did, because it was through moving the washing-tub off the stove that gave me the idea.”

“But where will you get the money from to buy a washing machine?”

“I’ll need four washing machines, not just one, and I’ll buy them on Hire Purchase.”

“Four washing machines, that’ll cost us a fortune. Are you sure this idea will work? We’ve just paid out a hundred pounds to buy the van.

“Yes I’m sure it will. Think it through for a minute. Think how much time and work you’ll save boiling, rubbing, rinsing, putting it through the wringer. So yes, I am positive it’ll work, I just can’t see it failing”

“What about customers, how will you go about getting those?”

"I'll go door to door around the housing estates canvassing, in the evenings after work. Once I've got enough people signed up, that'll be the time to go out and buy the four washing machines."

"Well, when you say it like that it does seem to make sense. Where are you thinking of canvassing?"

"I was thinking I'd start with Princess Drive first then Deysbrook Estate, Cantril Farm Estate and Gillmoss Estate, where my mother lives."

"Why choose Deysbrook Estate?"

"Because of the three story flats that are there."

"You mean you're going to carry heavy washing machines up and down stairs all day; why on earth would you want to do that?"

"Well, first of all, how many of those people do you think can afford a washing machine of their own? Very few, right?"

"Yes, ok, I'll go along with that."

"And secondly, because there aren't any Wash Houses in that area, they're forced to do their washing in the little boiler in the kitchen, just like everyone else who can't afford a washing machine. Just like you, your mother, and my mother - right?"

"Yes."

"And thirdly, I won't have to be lugging the washing machines up and down those stairs all day. I'll wheel them from one flat to the next. That's the advantage of serving the flats; lots of 'em in one place!"

"Ok, I can see the need. But you said yourself it still needs to be affordable for people to do it. How much will you charge?"

"I was thinking of charging three shillings an hour, like I just mentioned earlier, and maybe five shillings for a Saturday and Sunday.

"You've got it all worked out haven't you?"

"I think so, I've been working on it since half two this morning. I'm just hoping I've thought of everything. In fact, it's a good job we bought the van instead of a car, otherwise we'd have nothing to transport the machines around!"

"What if it doesn't work? What happens then? I'm expecting a baby don't forget; there'll only be one wage coming into the house in a few months."

"I know that, but I promise you, the moment I see it's not working out, I'll get myself another job right away. But honestly, I think it will. I just cannot see anyone refusing to hire one of those washing machines. Once they see how much easier their wash days are going to be, they'll want to hire one every week. All they'll have to do is fill it up with water, switch on the heater, sling in some washing powder and throw in the clothes. It's as simple as that. The machine will do the rest. What luxury is that? They'll think they've died and gone to heaven."

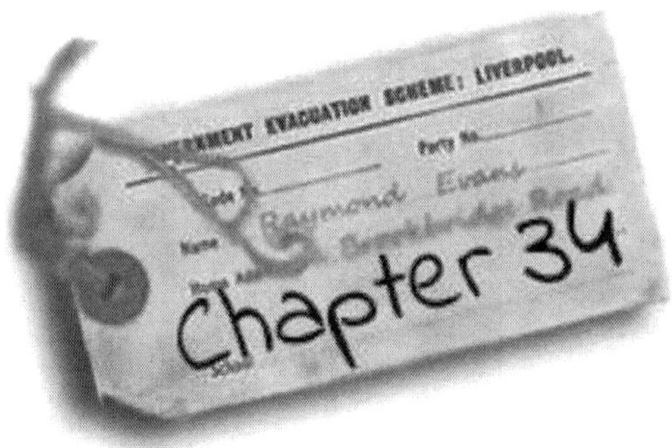

Discounts & Delivery Dates

The following three afternoons were taken up driving around Liverpool's city centre looking at different makes of washing machines, a job that turned out to be much more difficult than I'd expected. I knew absolutely nothing about washing and even less about washing machines. Had it not been for Lilian, I'd have finished up buying the wrong type of machine for sure. She explained that although they were more expensive it was important to get machines that had an internal water heater and an electric wringer. Anyway, it was the modern up-to-date 'Servis Washer' .The luxury 'MK17 Powerglide,' complete with its own water heater and wringer – two powered rollers on the top to squeeze the water out of the wet clothes.

washing with your

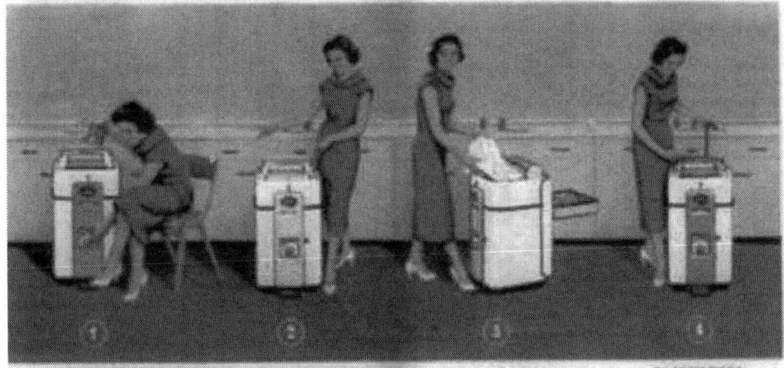

BOILING WASHING WRINGING EMPTYING

POWERGLIDE

EXCLUSIVE FOOT CONTROL

FREEDOM FOR BOTH HANDS

HEATER THAT BOILS

SNUGLY BUILT-IN WRINGER

SAFETY RELEASE BAR

ROLLERS SEPARATED

TURBULATOR AUTOMATICALLY CUTS OUT

PUSH-BUTTON CONTROL

SELF-EMPTYING PUMP

VITREOUS ENAMEL TUB

Owner's manual for the Servis Powerglide Washing Machines (Img. Source. Public Domain)

"It'll cost us a few pounds more, but it'll be well worth it," she said. "It's the type of machine I would like if I could afford it. It does everything you need it to do. It heats the water; rings the clothes out through the rollers and even drains the water out all by itself. It does everything. It'll make wash day a lot faster and easier than it's ever been before."

Once I'd explained that we were looking to buy four machines and not just one, I was able to quickly get the salesman to negotiate a substantial discount with the store manager. But I almost lost it again just as quickly when he realized I didn't plan to pay cash.

"I can't pay cash," I tell him. "It needs to be bought on Hire Purchase"

"I'll get the manager," he says, "just a moment."

A tall thin, anemic looking bloke sporting a Hitler hair cut comes striding out of his office with an anxious look on his face.

"I'm very sorry sir, but I can't allow you a discount, not when you're buying the machines on weekly payments."

"You can't? You mean I have to pay cash to get a discount, even though I'm buying four machines all at once?"

"Yes sir, that's the best price we can do when you're buying on payments."

"Okay. If you can't do it, you can't do it. I'll just have to go somewhere else. Thank you anyway, sorry to take up your time, goodbye."

"Just a moment sir, let's not get too hasty, let me think for a minute. Ah yes. I tell you what old chap; why don't you and your wife take a seat for a moment while I make a phone call to see if I can find a way to make this work? I won't keep you a minute."

We waited while Adolph made his phone call. It was only a few minutes before he sent the salesman over to ask us to join him in his office.

"Yes," he says, "I just got the go-ahead from head office approving the discount even though you'll be paying on hire purchase. But just so you know, they only approved it because you're buying four machines. Give me a few minutes while I get the papers together for you to sign."

"Sign up now? Oh no. I don't want to take them with me right now; I need another week."

"That's alright," the manager says, "It'll be best if we do the paperwork today, that way the discount is locked in.

But you can still pick the machines up next week when you're ready."

"No, I've just told you, I don't want to sign up, not right now. I haven't got the deposit with me anyway."

"What's that?" he almost shouted.

"You don't have the deposit? You mean you've come in here, in this store looking to purchase four washing machines without bringing any money with you? Well I never."

"Yes, that's right, I'm not ready to buy them just yet and I don't want to be paying for them until I'm ready to use them."

"Well I'm sorry sir, but the offer I've just made is only on the table for today, not next week!"

"I never said I'd be taking them with me today. I can't do that. But I will be back next week for them, most definitely, as long as you agree to hold the offer."

"But I could sell them in the meantime. How do I know if…"

"If I'll be back, is that what you were going to say? You'll just have to take my word for it. Please believe me; I need those machines more than you'll ever know. Just one week, that's all I'm asking for, you've got my word."

"You'll definitely be back in one week?"

"Yes, one week from today."

"Not a day longer?"

"One week from today, you've got my word."

I drove home happy and content knowing that everything was beginning to work out as planned.

"The most important thing now," I tell Lilian, "Is to use this week to get some customers lined up. In fact, I think I'll start canvassing tonight instead of tomorrow. I'll go and knock on some doors right after dinner."

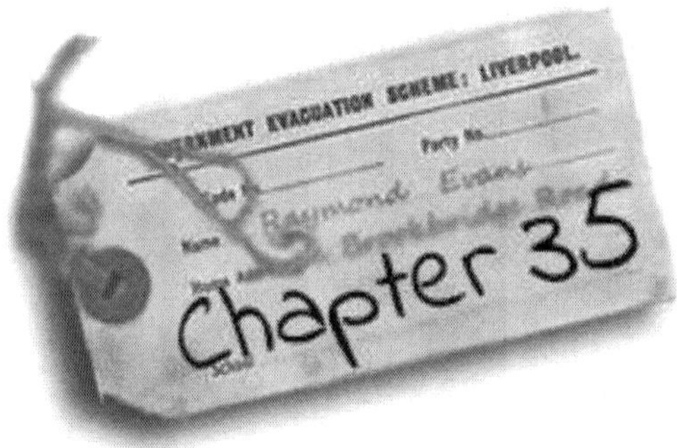

A Cold Night For Cold Calling

There were sparks coming off my knife and fork as I rushed my meal down. I desperately wanted to get a start on lining up some customers as quickly as possible. I had a nagging suspicion it may not be quite as easy as I'd thought.

"Do you think tonight's the right time?" Lilian asks, as I slip on my raincoat.

"It's much too late to be knocking on people's doors at this time of night, especially in this weather. It's getting on for seven o'clock."

"Maybe, but I want to get started. I can only canvass in the evenings after work, don't forget, and there's only six left between now and when I have to pick up the machines. That gives me six evenings to get at least eighty customers signed up. I'll sleep a lot more soundly tonight knowing I've got at least some customers under my belt."

"Are you sure you have enough time to do it all? Eighty customers is a lot to sign up. Maybe we should go back and ask that manager to give us a little longer?"

"No, there's no way I can do that! Adolph'll have a heart attack if I ask him to do that. And anyway, we'll lose the discount. Don't worry about it. Trust me; I will get eighty people signed up. I won't give up until I do. Listen, what woman in her right mind would want to continue to do her weekly wash in the way she's doing it now. I know my mother wouldn't, and neither would yours, right?"

"Yes, I suppose your right."

*****

Later that evening:

The weather was getting worse by the minute as I headed for Princess Drive's large council house estate, where I was fairly certain most of the tenants did not own a washing machine - *could even be as high as 90%,* I said to myself as I turned the corner.

"You'll only come home disappointed" I could hear Lilian saying, when I pulled up.

"Nobody wants to be standing on their door-step on a night like this. There's a gale force wind blowing out there, and it's just started sleeting."

I refused to listen. I wanted to at least give it a try.

So there I was, sitting in my little van outside someone's house, going over my sales pitch one more time, before getting out to knock on the lady's front door. It was based on something I'd read in one of the sales-books that belonged to my brother George when he worked as a brush salesman

I'd shortened and changed their corny spiel so I wouldn't be keeping the person waiting on the door-step for too long. The last thing I wanted was to have the door slammed in my face. It was a very simple pitch really:

'Sorry to trouble you at this time of night, I won't keep you long. I'm looking for people who'd be interested in hiring a washing machine to do their weekly wash. We'd deliver the machine, set it all up for you and come back an hour later to take it away. Is that something that would interest you?'

I jumped out of the van, made a dash along the path and rang the door bell at least three times, before someone finally decided to come to the door.

"Yes, what is it," a voice said from behind the closed door, "Who are you? What do you want?"

"I'm sorry to trouble you at this time of night, but..."

She opened the door, just a crack, took one look at me (I must've looked like the proverbial drowned rat but she went on…

> "Come back tomorrow," she said, before I had a chance to continue. "I do not intend standing here listening to you all night. Not in this weather. Not at this time of night."
>
> "I understand it's late, maybe I could speak to your husband then? It'll only take a minute."
>
> "Come back tomorrow" she said, "I don't want to listen to your twaddle - come back tomorrow."

BANG! She slams the door in my face.

Not wanting to throw in the towel so soon, I keep knocking until I hear heavy footsteps coming toward the door. I look through the letter-box and see a big heavy built man.

> "What's goin' on?" he says, in his deep Liverpool accent, "Who the bloody 'ell do yer think you are banging on our door like that?"
>
> "Sorry pal."
>
> "You're one of those Jehovah's Witness people aren't yer? They're the only people daft enough to come out in this bloody weather."
>
> "No, I'm not a Jehovah Witness."
>
> "Then who the 'ell are yer then? Wharris it yer want? Urry up man for God's sake, it's bloody freezing standin' ere!"

“I’m just trying to find out if your wife’s interested in hiring a washing machine, that’s all.”“Hire a washing machine, at this time of the bloody night? Ave yer just escaped from a lunatic asylum or somethin'? We’re goin' to bed in a minute.”

“No, no. Not right now. You don’t understand; I’m just canvassing for customers - that’s all.”

“Canvassin'?”

“Yes, canvassing,” I tell him, reaching into my pocket. “Why don’t you let me step inside out of the rain so I can show this photo of the washing machine, it’ll only take a minute – please, I’m getting soaked out here.”

“Alright then, but just for a minute.”

“That’s it there, see? That machine you’re looking at will do all the week’s washing in just ONE short hour. By the way, how long does your wife **normally** take to do the washing?”

“How long does me wife take to do the washin', ow the ‘ell should I know? I don’t do the bloody washin', do I?”

“Well, whatever time it does take her, I guarantee she’ll have it done in half the time, I can promise you that. Then all she’ll have to do is hang it out to dry.”

“Have yer been anywhere else, like ‘er next door?”

“No not yet, you’re the first I’ve canvassed around here.”

“You mean we’re yer **very** first customer?”

“Yes.”

“Yer berra cum through to the lounge and talk to the Missus, I think she just might be interested.”

“Thanks.”

“Just listen to im luv. Lerr im explain while I go in the kitchen and make uz a nice hot cup of tea. I think yer’ll like what he’s got to say. It sounds a lot better idea than strugglin' with that old boiler in the kitchen.”

“I’m not trying to sell you a washing machine,” I tell his wife who’s sitting by the fire in a thick fluffy dressing gown puffing heavily on a cigarette.

“I’m just trying to find out if you’re interested in hiring one, that’s all. Here’s a photo, have a look at it while I explain how much easier it’ll make your wash days by using one of these machines.

“For a start, you’ll not have to boil the water to wash the clothes anymore, or scrub them on a washing board to get the dirt out. You won’t even have to rinse, squeeze or put them through the old wringer, ever again. All the hard work will be done by this electronically driven washing machine you’re now looking at.”

“Well that all sounds very nice lad, but how much will it cost me?”

“Three shillings an hour, Missus.”

"And it heats the water? Is that what yer sayin', it actually heats the water?"

"Yes."

"All on its own?"

"Yes Missus, it heats the water all on its own."

"How does the wringer work then, can't see any 'andle in this 'ere photo?"

"It doesn't work like your old wringer, missus. Those rollers you're looking at do the work for you. They're powered by electricity. All you have to do is press this lever here at the base of the machine and the rollers will squeeze all the water out of the clothes for you. Can you see it? Put your glasses on, you'll be able to see much better."

"So let's get this right. What you're saying is, that every time I want to put somethin' through the mangle, I'm sorry, I mean the rollers, I just have to press that lever down, that one at the bottom of the machine I'm luckin at."

"Yes, missus."

"With me foot?"

The woman's a genius!

"Yes, missus, with your foot."

“What if I haven’t finished when yer come to collect the machine? I mean, I’ve never used one of these new-fangled things before, it might take me a bit to get used to it”

“You can hire it for longer if you like, just as long as you tell me before-hand. But if there’s only you and your husband, you’ll only need it for one hour anyway, that’s all it takes my wife to do our full weeks washing.”

“It all sounds too good to be true; what days will yer be cumin around?”

“Mondays around here Missus, will that suit you?”

“Mornins or afternoons?”

“Whichever you choose.”

“Can yer come in the afternoon, round about three, when me ‘usband’s ‘ome from werk? He’s more technical minded than me.”

More technically minded...you don’t say!

“Yes Missus, no problem. Now then, are you ready to sign up?”

“Yes, of course I’d like to sign up. By the way are yer goin' next door? I’m sure she’ll want to hire one as well. She’s gorra a tribe of kids to wash for, eight as a matter of fact, and all going to school as well.”

“Yes, I’m going there right now.”“Good, tell her Maggie from next door sent yer.”

"I will Missus, thanks. Cheerio then!"

I stuck at the canvassing for two more hours before deciding it was time to pack up, go home, get out of my wet clothes and have a nice hot cup of tea in front of the fire. But I did manage to get eleven signed up, which I thought was pretty good considering the weather. It certainly wasn't the kind of night for anyone to want to be standing on their door-step listening with a fifty mile an hour gale-force wind blowing down their hallway.

In fact, because of the bad weather, quite a few refused to even open their front door. They preferred speaking through their letter box instead. Some would apologize and politely ask me to come back tomorrow, while others on the other hand told me in no uncertain manner to go away - or words to that effect. I made a note of the nicer ones who asked me to come back tomorrow by scribbling their house numbers on the back of my note pad.

Except for the house with the Great Dane, that is, I definitely wasn't going back there, ever! The dog's loud bark was the reason I bent down to look through the letter box. I was really I glad I did, because I saw a frail skinny little man being dragged up the hallway by the biggest dog I'd ever seen. The determination on this very strong and powerful animal's face said he wanted me for his dinner. And it was easy to see he had the strength to bash down the front door and grab hold of me before I was able to even make it to the front gate. I was terrified. I could picture myself being ravaged in the middle of the road listening to the skinny little man shouting at the top of his voice:

> **“Rusty, you naughty boy, put him down right now, right this minute!"**

At that point I decided to call it a night. I’d managed to sign up 11 and that was just as many players as Liverpool need towin a match. So I decided that was going to be my lucky number and headed home, very wet, a little bit weary but massively excited all at the same time.

> “You look like a drowned rat,” Lilian said, as I peeled off my soggy wet clothes, “How did you get on?”
>
> “The weather was a problem like you said it would be, otherwise I’m certain I’d have got a lot more signed up. But I did manage to get eleven to sign up. That leaves me needing just sixty nine more to reach my goal of eighty. If I can average twelve new customers each day for the next six days, we’ll be all set.”

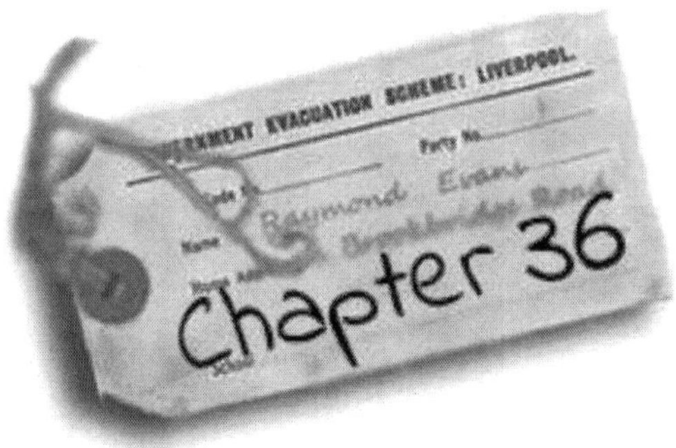

Breakdowns Are Getting Me Down

Dateline: Three months later.

Although the business is making good money, it's beginning to get more and more difficult getting around all eighty customers on time. Chiefly because, a good percentage of the customers (those with large families for instance) are never finished on time. Consequently, I'm always late getting to the next customer. In fact, there have been a lot of little problems arising lately – unforeseen niggling little problems.

I have to go to the Deysbrook council estate this weekend and tell the customers who live in those second and third storey flats that I'll not be bringing them a washing machine anymore. I'm dreading it. I feel so sorry for them. I feel I'm letting them down. I should've listened to Lilian; then none of this would be happening. She did warn me about canvassing the Deysbrook

Council Estate, about the problems they were having with the Lifts. About them breaking down all the time because of the kids riding up and down in them all day long. I'll just have to tell those people there's no way I can carry on lugging these heavy washing machines up and down six flights of stairs every single day. I'll be in a wheelchair before I know it.

*****

There are more problems on my very next pick-up.

It's as if a tsunami has passed through her kitchen, water everywhere, all the way along the lobby right up to the front door.

"I left it filling while I went for me daughter," she says. "She lives across the street so I let her use it as well. She's got three small kids. When I got back, the water was cumin' out all over the place. I couldn't stop it no how. Look how deep it is in here? It's nearly up to me ankles. I'm sorry Ray but I don't want a machine anymore, it's far too complicated. I'm really scared to use it. I mean I could've been electrocuted. Water and electricity don't mix, you do know that don't you? And look at me Lino, it's completely ruined. The water's gone right through to the floor boards. I'm dread'n me 'usband comin 'ome. He'll go stark raving mad when he sees this lot."

Then there was the lady who thought it would be a good idea to put her dirty dishes in the machine when she'd finished her washing. I'm not making this up, I actually caught her doing it, when I called back to pick up the machine. There she was, carefully lowering the last of her dirty breakfast dishes down into the brown murky water. It looked like it was the same water she'd washed the baby's nappies in. Yuck!

"You can't do that," I tell her, "you can't put the dishes in there."

"And why not," she says, "It'll not do them any harm?"

"Of course it will," I tell her, "they'll be smashed to pieces."

"Don't be silly," she says, looking at me like I'm a little retarded. "You don't think I'm that daft do you? Good God man, I'm not that stupid. You don't really think I'm going to switch the machine on with the dishes inside, do you? I'm just giving them a good soak in the hot water to get the grease off, that's all. I always put them in there

when I've finished doing the washing. It's a shame to waste all that hot water!"

Everything seemed to be going wrong all at the same time. Like the day I stopped by my mothers' for a quick cup of tea. We were sitting at the table quietly chatting when my young brother David came flying through the door:

"Hey Ray! I just saw some fella going around canvassing

your customers. He's charging them sixpence an hour less than you're charging."

"Where, Dave? Where did you see him?"

"He's around the corner in Altcross Road talking to one of your customers."

I jumped up and drove over to find out who might have the audacity to try to steal my customers. I arrived just as he was loading his machine into his aging Robin Reliant van. He seemed to be a well-mannered young lad about seventeen or eighteen. He apologized saying the lady had approached him about hiring the machine because he was charging sixpence an hour less than I was. He said it didn't matter to her that his machine didn't have a water heater or electric rollers; a shilling a week was a lot of money to her.

"A shilling," I said, "you mean she kept the machine for two hours?" "Yes," he said, "she's got a husband and six kids."

"You sound like you know a lot about her, do you live around here?"

"I do," he said, pointing upwards," I live way up there in that flat with me Gran. I know everyone around here."

His grandmother was leaning over the balcony trying to catch the conversation.

"Well you might as well have all the customers in these flats," I said, "I've had enough of climbing stairs anyway."

His face lit up in disbelief.

"Are you serious? I can have all of them?"

"Yes," I said, "all of them."

"Would you mind nipping up the stairs and telling me Gran what you just said? She was worried there might be trouble when I started this up."

"Okay," I said," but I can't stay too long, I've got my machines to pick up."

She seemed like a nice old lady. She thanked me for being so understanding and went on to ask, if I ever decided on selling up, would I give her grandson first refusal on buying the rest of the business from me.

*****

I'm sitting in a lady's kitchen one day drinking a cup of tea, waiting for her to finish emptying the machine when she says:

"I'm sorry to keep you waiting Ray, I know I'm always late finishing, but we have so much washing to do. Is there any possible way you could let me have the machine for two hours in future instead of just the one. My daughter wants to use it as well. I'll pay the difference?"

"Yes, of course you can have it for two hours, just as long as you let me know in advance. I'll work something out."

"But what about the next customer after me, won't it make you late with her machine?"

"Don't worry, I can sort that out. In fact, thinking about it, you've just given me an idea."

"What do you mean?"

"Well, instead of charging you double, six shillings for the two hours, how about if I knocked the price down a little and charged you five shillings? That way, it'll only cost you and your daughter just two shillings and sixpence each."

"Abso-bloody-lutely," she says, "That's even better. So starting from next week, I get the machine for two hours instead of just the one?"

"Yes."

"Every Wednesday?"

"Yes."

"The same time you bring it now?"

"Yes, I'll book you down for two hours every Wednesday starting from next week?"

"You won't let me down now will you? I couldn't go back to doing the washing like I used to. Not anymore."

"No, of course I won't let you down. Like I just said, you've given me a great idea."

Having dropped off all four machines, I spent the next hour sitting in the van with a note-pad on my knee figuring out the best way to make it work. I showed it to Lilian when I got home to see what she thought of my little brain-wave.

"I think I'll try getting all the customers to do the same thing," I told her. "I'll try talking them into keeping the machine for two hours instead of just the one."

"But some of them may not be able to afford the extra money. What if they can't afford to pay the extra two shillings?"

"I'll just have to explain that I can't go on doing it the way I'm doing it now. It's not working out. I'm letting too many people down by getting to them too late, just because others are running over their time. They're going to have to take the machine for two hours or not have it at all."

"How long has this been going on; getting around late? You've not mentioned it before."

"It all started a few weeks ago when some of the customers began going over their allotted time. Last Thursday I was so far behind, by the end of the day the last few customers were refusing to take the machine from me. I've been losing as much as six, sometimes twelve shillings a day. I think the customers will understand, most of them will, anyway. I'm sure they won't want to go back to washing their clothes the way they used to - at the wash house or in the kitchen sink."

*****

The changeover cut my work rate in half. It not only made life much easier, but cut out all the lost rental time. The extra profit helped me pay off the last of the hire purchase agreement much sooner.

My total takings now (including the sale of washing powder and blocks of soap) were averaging around twenty eight to thirty pounds a week, about a hundred and ten to a hundred and twenty pounds a month. That was a substantial amount of money in those days. To give you some idea what I mean by that, the average working man's wage in Britain in the 50s and 60s was around five pounds (£5) a week.

Things continued to plod along nicely after the changeover. In fact, having so much extra time on my hands, I even considered buying a couple more washing machines. It was just as well I didn't, because that very same week two of the machines broke down - the electric motors had over-heated, and burnt themselves out. I had learned to fix minor things on the machines myself, but when a motor burned out there was nothing I could do but haul it back to the workshop and have a new motor fitted, which to my horror, cost nearly half as much as I'd paid for the washing machine in the first place.

> "You bought the wrong machines mate," the engineer told me, "these machines were made for normal household use, one or two hours a week. They're certainly not built to run sixty hours a week!"

After talking it over with Lilian, it was decided I should pull out and get myself a job before it was too late. Financial problems were the last thing I wanted; especially with another mouth to feed. So the next day I drove over to young Syd Bailey's house.

Syd's Grandma, a nice old lady, opened the door and led me down the hall into the kitchen where her grandson was at the table enjoying a plate of fish and chips. I reminded her she'd asked me to give Syd first refusal if I ever decided to sell the business.

"It depends how much you want for the business," she said, "because it'll be me putting up the money.

I'm the only family Syd's got now. His Mum and Dad were killed in the blitz when he was just a child."

"Well the least I can sell it to you for is eighty pounds, twenty pounds for each machine."

"Does that include everything?" asks Syd.

"What do you mean by everything?

"Good Will," his Grandma says, "That's what he means. Are you going to charge him anything for Good Will?"

"No. The eighty pounds includes everything, except the van of course."

"What do you think Gran?" he said, turning to his grandmother, "Will you help me? I can make a go of it, I know I can."

"If you don't mind me asking," grandma says, "but how much did the machines cost you originally?"

"Just over fifty pounds each, plus interest. I can show you the invoice if you like. By the way three of them, have just been fitted with brand new motors."

The deal was done. A fortnight later grandma gave me a cheque for £80.00 plus £90 for the van which went towards a used car not long after. A car I should add, that gave me no **end** of trouble but I'll tell you about that later

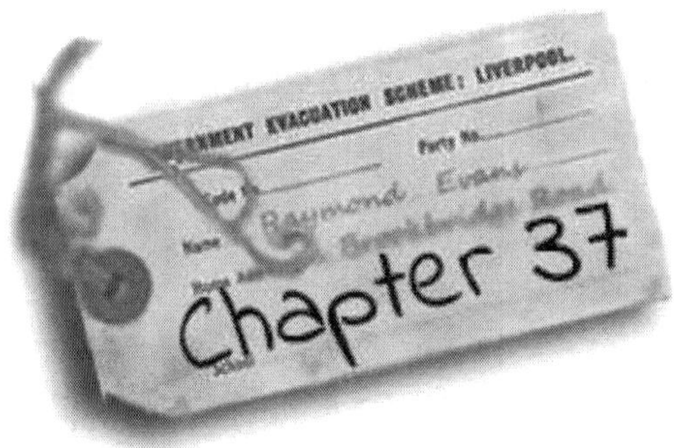

Bread Run & Rum Run

Dateline: Summer, 1957.

It was in the summer of 1957, a month or so after our son Raymond was born, I started working for George Lunt Ltd. An old established family Bakery business that stretched back into the mid eighteen hundreds.

I was still feeling a little disheartened having failed to make more of the washing machine business than I did. My hopes of making enough money to start up a launderette business (which was the ultimate plan) had long gone out of the window. Anyway, there was nothing I could do about it now: my main concern was providing for my wife and our new son.

I was put on a flat rate of £6.00 a week and promised a route of my own when one became available. However, had I known beforehand how long it normally took for a salesperson to get a route of his own, I would not have accepted the job in the first place. I'd have looked elsewhere. As things turned out, it was just as well I didn't know about that, because after only a few months, three maybe four at the most, the sales manager Mr. Taylor called me into his office one afternoon and offered me one of the largest routes in the company. The route covered an area from Birkenhead all the way along the Wirral Peninsula through to Ellesmere Port. I couldn't believe my luck. I was truly flabbergasted. I couldn't understand why he chose me above the two other people waiting for a route, they'd both been with the company far longer than I had.

> "It's not an easy route," he said, "It's very spread out, you'll have thirty one shops, two small Cottage Hospitals, and two sizeable cafés to serve each day. Your route starts in Conway Street in Birkenhead, just after leaving the Mersey Tunnel and finishes on the other side of Ellesmere Port. So to get around on time; you must leave the bakery no later than five thirty each morning, much earlier than anyone else. As you've probably learned already, it's very important you're never late getting round to your customers. Otherwise they won't hesitate to buy their bread and cakes from our competitors. And if that happens, you'll lose the route immediately - no excuses. You will be fired on the spot. This is a highly competitive business. You'll have at least three or four other companies to contend with every single day, all fighting for the same shelf space. So don't let me down by showing up late. That was the problem with the last salesman. So what do you think? Do you think you're up to it?

"Yes. I can do that, no problem."

"Right, let me ask you another question. Do you think you can build the route up even higher than it is now?"

"Yes. I've done that kind of thing before."

"That was a very quick response Ray, are you sure?

"Yes, I am sure. I did that same route just last week when Bert was sent home for coming in late. One of the supervisors came with me to show me the way around."

"Yes, I know, he told me. In fact it was that same supervisor who suggested I should consider you for the route."

"So when do you want me to start?"

"You can start tomorrow. Peter will be your van boy. He's been on that same route for over a year now. He came here straight from school. So he knows it inside out, and more importantly, he's never late. I want you to look after this kid. He's honest and he's a hard worker, so please treat him right."

I couldn't wait to get home to tell Lilian the good news, that I'd been trusted with one of the top earning routes in the whole company. If I worked hard and was able to build the sales even higher than they are now, it wouldn't be too long before we would be able to move out of the flat and buy a place of our own; one with a little garden even.

"Let's wait and see," she said, "Let's take one step at a time. I know how much you want us to have a place of our own, and I know you won't be happy until we get it, but I'm happy renting just now. I just don't want you killing yourself."

She was always saying things like that, she still does. She's a kind hearted gentle person who never complains about anything; just gets on with life and accepts what comes along.

"Oh, by the way, while we're on the subject of houses, my mother was talking to one of the neighbors the other day about us wanting to move out of the flat and rent a house. Her neighbor said her sister's getting divorced and her ex-husband is looking for someone to share his house. He wants someone who can help him with the rent because it'll be too much for him on his own. She says it's a really nice house with three good size bedrooms, a parlor, a dining room, a kitchen, a bathroom and toilet upstairs and nice gardens back and front."

"Where is it?" I asked.

"Abingdon Road, off Walton Hall Avenue."

"How much is he asking for the rent?"

"Two pounds a month, that's all"

"That's only a few shillings more than we're paying now in this tiny little flat; it sounds really fair to me. Let's go and have a look at it."

We moved in a fortnight later.

all I want is a peaceful world and a pork pie!

*****

Sam Hudson, a lean average height sixty three year old had worked on Liverpool Docks for close on fifty years. He couldn't wait for his retirement day to arrive. The days of being able to potter around the garden, take a stroll over to the Stanley Arms Pub for a pint of Bitter and a game of darts. Or just settle down in his armchair with a good book and a few tots of his ***very strong*** Jamaican Rum. It all couldn't come fast enough.

You may wonder why I've given emphasis to both the words 'very' and 'strong'. Well, it wasn't just the normal run-of-the-mill Rum you get in a bar or a pub. This was the real McCoy. One-hundred percent proof that tasted like, well, fire water.

One evening, not long after we moved in, Sam knocked on the parlor door and asked if I'd like to join him for a drink.

> "Sure Sam, that'd be nice" I said, following him into the lounge.

> "Ever had real Rum before Ray? I'm guessing probably not, this is the real McCoy," he said, reaching into the cupboard for his bottle of Rum.

I've never been much of a drinker and the idea of drinking shots of Rum already had me a little worried.

> "Do you mind if I have a beer instead Sam? I'm not all that keen on spirits."

His face fell.

"Just give it a try Ray," he said, "You might like it. It's not that cheap stuff they dish out in the pub. Like I just said, this is the real McCoy, a hundred percent proof."

"Well, alright then, but just a small one."

"A small one" Is that all you want, just a small one? You can do better than that Ray? It is my birthday today, don't forget."

"Oh, so it is. Sorry Sam, I forgot."

"That's ok. I wasn't expecting you to remember."

"Whoa take it easy Sam; I'll never drink all that."

"How do you know you won't, you said you'd never tasted Rum before? You might like it."

"I know, but there's enough in there for six people."

"Just swig it down Ray for God's sake. Anyone would think it was a dose of medicine I was giving you."

"Jesus."

"What?"

"Nothing, just thinking out loud, that's all."

We sat for a while chatting, Sam stretching his neck every now and then to check on my glass.

"Come on Ray," he said, rising from his chair, "speed up, you've hardly drunk any. There's plenty more where that came from. I'm on my third already."

"I'm drinking it as fast as I can Sam."

"Tell you what Ray. I'm going up to the toilet. When I get back, I'd really like to see that glass of yours empty. If it is, I'll let you have a bottle of the Mann's Brown Ale you were asking about before, fair-enough? Looking at your glass, you're nearly halfway there anyway."

"Okay Sam, that's a deal."

I was up off the couch like a shot the moment he closed the door looking around for somewhere to dump the rest of my drink. I glanced over at the giant rubber plant that was sitting in the corner of the room.

No, no, bad idea, it might kill it! Oh God, What am I going to do? I can't drink the rest of this stuff, it tastes like brake fluid.

I heard the toilet being flushed so I closed my eyes ready to gulp down the rest of the rum when I suddenly I thought about the fireplace. I rushed over and emptied what was left in my glass onto the dead ashes, or what I thought were dead ashes. WHOOSH! A mini explosion, followed by a huge cloud of hot ash shot out from the fireplace covering me practically from head to toe, just as Sam came back into the room.

"What the hell happened?" Sam asked. "Are you alright?"

"Yes, I think so."

"Don't tell me you threw your drink on the fire, Ray, surely not?"

I couldn't bring myself to tell him the truth.

"No. I was just poking around when I accidently spilled just a little of the rum onto the ashes."

"Good God man, it's all over you," he said. "Are you sure you're ok? Are you burnt anywhere?"

"No, I'm okay; it just feels a bit warm that's all."

"I'm sorry," he said, trying his best to hide the grin on his face."

"But you look quite funny covered in all that ash. Go look at yourself in the mirror; anyone would think a bloody Zombie had just walked into the room. Here, give me your glass while I fill it up again."

There is more to this story, but for the life of me, I can't remember any of it!

all I want is a peaceful world and a pork pie!

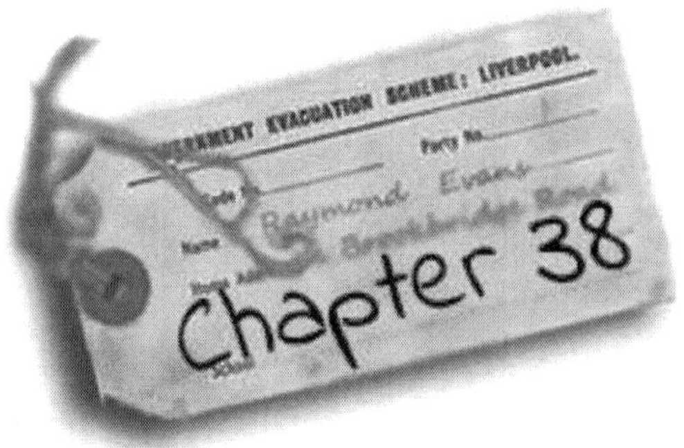

Hot Cross Bun Battles

Anyway, getting back to the George Lunt story, the sales manager was absolutely right about Pete, the van boy. I arrived in work the very next morning to find Pete already busying himself at the back of the delivery van, making up the first six orders, just like he'd always done for Bert. I thanked him for coming in early to do that.

"We're going to make a good team, Pete" I said, as I began maneuvering the van out of the bakery yard, "You work hard for me and I'll make sure you're well rewarded, fair enough? The more commission I make, the more money I'll be able to pass onto you at the end of the week."

"That's ok by me," he said, "thanks very much."

Let me just explain, why some shopkeepers in those days, often found it difficult to strike up a good working relationship with their bread delivery people. The salesmen were delivering a commodity that brought customers into a store, but only gave the shopkeeper a miserly 12.5% profit. It also took up a considerable amount of shelf space, leaving less room for more profitable goods.

The shopkeeper's only consolation (if you could call it that) was that no matter which company he chose to purchase his bread from, it was always sold on a sale or return basis. Bread was a staple of most people's diet in those days, so they wanted to be able to get it fresh daily along with other staples. So if a store was going to attract customers, they needed to have the basics covered, even if it had to be at a low profit margin. The shopkeepers then had to hope they could make up by selling more profitable goods once they had the customer inside their store.

So every day was a race against the clock trying to get around your customers on time. Bread salesmen in those days were always being pulled by the police for driving beyond the speed limit. I know; I was one of them. Arriving at a shop late meant losing out on sales. Shopkeepers worrying you may or may not show up would eventually simply buy more from your competitors who were already in the store. Whenever that happened it would seriously affect your commission.

There was always friendly competition amongst the "bread boys". But as is often the case in life, one or two took it just that bit too far. One of my main competitors was the guy who worked for 'Mother's Pride' Bakeries. A short, wily little fellow who drove his bread van through the sleepy Wirral villages at speeds Niki

Lauda would have been proud of. No one liked this little fellow. He had no consideration for anyone but himself. He simply refused to abide by the 'unwritten rules'. The man was never satisfied keeping to the shelf space he was allocated, he'd just pile his bread on top of everyone else's so his would sell first. It wasn't unusual to walk into one of your shops the next day and find most of your bread buried way down underneath his, squashed and flattened like a pile of pancakes. He was always 'burying' everyone else's bread, which was why we nick-named him, 'The Undertaker'. He had all sorts of conniving tricks up his sleeve. Like the time he sneaked into my van and stole my 'Dragging Iron,' a long hooked metal pole that was used to drag the bread trays to the back of the van. Having to climb inside the van at every delivery to pull the heavy stacks of bread trays forward, not only made the job more difficult, but it also made you very late getting around and losing out on sales, and commission. ALL the bread boys hated the 'Undertaker.'

I was driving along a narrow winding country lane one dark and drizzly wintry morning when the 'Undertaker' suddenly appeared in my mirror trying his best to overtake. His intentions were to pass me and get to Clegg's Mini-Market before I did. To tell Mr. Clegg I was running late and that he should buy a few extra trays of bread from him. It was a dangerous move he was making, the road was greasy and there were a lot of sharp bends ahead. Not wanting to take any chances, I let him go past. It was just as well, because about a half mile further on, I arrived just in time to see his van zigzagging in the middle of the road trying to avoid a herd of cows coming out of the farmer's yard. 'The Undertaker' lost control and skidded across the road before crashing through the fence. He did manage to avoid the farmer and the cows so no one was hurt. The upside for me was, I not only doubled my bread sales that day, but I sold out of confectionary as well. I had no choice but to tell his customers what had happened. That the 'Undertaker' was sitting in his van in the middle of the farmer's field up to his running boards in mud. The assumption being that it would be quite some time before he would show up.

*****

There was one particular customer on that bread route that I'll never forget until the day I die, and that was Mr. Grimshaw, a short, snooty pompous ex military man who never failed to find something to complain about. Let me give you just one example as to why I hated dealing with this person. Why I woke each and every day dreading the thought of having to listen to his never ending complaints. Why I hated everything about him, including his la-di-dah wife and their yappy little Jack Russell terrier; that delighted in snapping at my heels the moment I walked into their shop.

Not a day went by without Mr. Grimshaw and his overbearing dictatorial wife complaining about something or other. One of their choice gripes was about the local council passing planning permission for a mini-supermarket to be built quite near to his shop. He was always complaining and going on about that. In fact I can hear him now as I write:

"Every single one of those councilors should be put against a wall and shot. Who the hell do they think they are, allowing foreigners to come over here and open shops, where and whenever they want - taking the bread and butter out of our mouths?"

He may have had a point if the mini-market he was referring to was erected right next door, but it was at least a mile away, if not more.

Easter was one of those holiday weekends that made for a great bonus if you could increase sales of both bread and confectionary, but you still had to get around your route in about the same time as you normally did.

It was around eleven fifteen on a Thursday morning when I arrived at his shop; a week prior to the Easter bank holiday.

"What's this Evans?" he said, jabbing his stubby little finger at his watch, "You're late!"

"I'm sorry Mr. Grimshaw, but it's only a quarter past eleven, we're not **THAT** late. Just fifteen minutes, that's all."

"You're late just the same! Some of these ladies have been waiting **ages** for you, isn't that right my dears?" he said, gesturing toward two elderly ladies behind him.

The ladies didn't say anything, just looked shocked listening to him berating me.

"Oh it doesn't matter Mr. Grimshaw," another lady shouted, "we're not in that much of hurry."

"Maybe so my dear, but I do have a business to run you know. I've got to look after my customers; otherwise before I know it, you'll be taking your custom elsewhere. There's a lot more competition around here now. I need to take care of my regulars. I can't have the likes of him keeping you waiting every day.

"But I'm almost never late unless there's been an accident or something. And besides, these ladies prefer Lunt's products, and I don't serve any other shops around here," I said.

"And you'd better not," he said, raising his voice, "otherwise you'll be for the high jump sonny, make no mistake about that!"

"Would you please give me your hot-cross bun order Mr. Grimshaw? Today's the last day I can accept orders. I did remind you last week. The Bakery needs to have our orders in no later than five o'clock today, so they can set up the bake and work schedules."

"I'll give you my hot cross bun order when I'm good and ready," he snapped back.

"But Mr. Grimshaw, I keep telling you, I have to have my hot-cross bun orders in by five o'clock today. I've got everyone else's orders. This is the very last day for ordering. If I don't hand your order in when I get back to the bakery, I won't have any hot-cross buns on the van for you. It is Easter next week, don't forget."

“You don’t have to tell me when Easter is, sonny. And I don’t care what your bakery says, I’ve ordered my hot cross buns from Scotts Bakeries, like I’ve always done for as long as I can remember, for as long as I’ve had this shop as a matter of fact. He gets here long before you do.”

“So you don’t want any from me then?”

“Not unless you can get here at the same time as the Scotts salesman always does, seven o’clock, on-the-dot! First come, first served, that’s what I always say.”

“I keep telling you Mr. Grimshaw, I’m miles away from here at that time of the morning. I’m on the other side of Birkenhead. I can’t be at every shop at the same time Mr. Grimshaw, that’s impossible.”

“Then you’ll just have to lose out on your commission won’t you, because that what’s really bothering you, isn’t it?”

“No, it’s not the commission I’m concerned about, it’s having to refuse you if you run out which is what happened last year, don’t forget, when you didn’t order enough from Scotts. The bakery doesn’t allow returns on confectionary, so I won’t be carrying any extras because what I take back comes out of my pocket. Surely you understand that Mr. Grimshaw? I’m not trying to be awkward; it’s just that they’ll take the money out of my wages if I return any confectionary items.”

"I don't care. I'll not be ordering any hot cross buns from your company this year; I've got plenty coming from the Scotts salesman."

"That's okay Mr. Grimshaw, just as long we understand each other. It's just that I don't want to have to refuse you when I get here next Thursday morning. Don't forget, there are no deliveries until the Tuesday after Easter, you do know that, don't you?"

"I know, and I'm telling you, I've ordered plenty of everything from Scotts. I'll have more than enough hot-cross buns to last me right through the bank holiday. All I need from you is my usual order of three dozen thin sliced loaves, one dozen thick sliced loaves, three dozen jam doughnuts, and two dozen custard tarts, just like I always get from you."

*****

It was around eleven o 'clock on the following Thursday morning when I pulled up outside grumpy Grimshaw's shop, the day before Good Friday. And just like all the other shops I'd served on that particular morning, his little store was crammed to the door with customers, pushing and jostling each other wanting to fill their baskets with bread, groceries and freshly baked hot-cross buns. It was a typical Easter Bank Holiday weekend, people shopping as if they were stocking up for an impending famine.

"Thank God you're here," Mrs. Grimshaw says, as Pete and I push our way through to the counter.

"I was beginning to think you'd never get here. These good people have been waiting over an hour for you to arrive. Where have you been until now?"

"Where have WE been?" Peter says, "This is the time we normally get here Mrs. Grimshaw, we're always here right around eleven o'clock."

"Well, never mind that now," she says, as Pete lowers a tray of bread onto the counter, "I need twelve dozen hot cross buns as well as my usual order. We've been sold out since ten o'clock this morning."

I can't describe how exasperating and infuriating it was to have to stand there listening to her demands. This rude and difficult woman couldn't even bring herself to admit that her husband had made a mistake. To at least apologize and say she was sorry, to ask if I could possibly help them out? That would have made all the difference.

"I'm sorry, but I don't have any spares Mrs. Grimshaw," I said. "Your husband didn't order any hot-cross buns from me. I've just enough left for my last few shops."

"I'll go out to the van," her husband says. "Take no notice of him; I'll make sure we get some."

"There's no point," I tell him, "There's no need for you to go out there, I can't let you have any, they're all ordered - and it's locked up anyway."

"What do you mean," he says, "they're all ordered? I have customers here waiting for hot-cross- buns, now go out to the van and get me some this minute, before I get on the phone and call your boss."

"That's right," his wife says, "Get his boss on the phone."

"The duty supervisor wants to speak to you," he says, handing me the phone. "Come and speak to him. I hope he fires you."

"Hello."

"Can't you give him a few just to keep him happy?"

"I REALLY don't want to."

"What do you mean you don't want to? He was going crazy on the phone just then. You need to do something to help him out."

"Like what? He flatly refused to give me an order."

"You must have ordered a few extras? A couple of hundred or so, all the other salesmen have."

"I did. I ordered an extra five hundred, but I've sold most of them, might have about seven or eight dozen left, that's all."

"Then give him some those, for God's sake."

"No. I don't feel like I should, I've got other customers who don't abuse me every day like he does. I'm sick of the way he and his wife treat me and Pete. I'm not taking it anymore."

"You do know what will happen if you refuse to serve him, don't you? You'll not only lose your route, but you'll lose your job as well."

I slammed the phone down. I'd had enough. I wanted to get out of the shop away from Mr. Grimshaw, his wife and their bad tempered snarling dog.

"Where are you going?" Mr. Grimshaw shouts, "Where are going with my bread and my doughnuts?"

"You're not getting anything from me today Mr. Grimshaw, bread, doughnuts, custard tarts or hot-cross buns. Get 'Scotts' on the phone and ask them to bring you some. I've had enough of you and your wife. Come on Pete, let's get out of here."

"DON'T YOU WALK AWAY FROM ME, COME BACK HERE RIGHT NOW! I NEED THAT BREAD. I NEED IT FOR THESE PEOPLE WHO'VE HAVE BEEN WAITING. DO YOU HEAR ME?"

I apologized to the customers on my way out of the shop and suggested they buy their bread and hot-cross buns from the new mini-market down the road.

"I'm on my way there right now," I tell them, "They've been asking me to serve them ever since they opened. So I won't be coming back here again."

"What do you think will happen when we get back," Pete asks, "Do you think they WILL sack you?" "Not sure what they'll do Pete. Either that or they'll take me off the route. I shouldn't have done what I did, I know, but I couldn't help it. I've run out of patience with that pair. I've put up with them long enough. Why do they always have to talk down to us every time we walk into their shop? Why can't they be a little more civil? It's not my fault I lost my temper."

It was five o'clock when I finally arrived back at the bakery. Everybody had left except one of the office girls and the duty supervisor. I'd just finished cashing- in and making out my bread orders, when the supervisor pulled me to one side to tell me about Mr. Graham wanting to see me in his office on Tuesday morning; that someone else will be doing my route that day.

"I think it'll be very un-fair of Mr. Graham if he takes the route away from me," I tell the supervisor, "at least he should listen to my side of the story first."

"You shouldn't have done what you did," the supervisor says. "You know the rules. You've no excuse. Lose a customer and you lose your job."

"Do you think he'll sack me?"

"Yes I do. He was fuming when I told him what had happened, that you refused the customer his order."

Everything had been being going along so nicely. I was top salesman, making really good money, more than enough to put an extra few pounds aside towards a deposit on a house. Something that Lilian didn't even know about. I wanted it to be a surprise. Now it looked like all those plans were going out the window.

What am I going to tell her? I kept asking myself as I drove home. How do I tell her I've not only lost my route, but may lose my job as well? I shouldn't have done what I did - shouldn't have lost my temper.

*****

Tuesday Morning:

It was near to ten o'clock when Mr. Graham's secretary called me into his office. I'd been standing outside for close on an hour praying he would change his mind, hoping he would at least listen to my side of the story, and possibly give me another chance. But judging by the look on his face as I walked in, it wasn't looking too good.

"What the hell happened last Thursday?" he asked, "refusing your customer his order."

"I'm sorry, I know it was wrong. It won't happen again."

"Do you know what happened after you drove away from his shop?"

"No."

"Your supervisor called me. I had to drive over there in my car and deliver it myself."

"I'm sorry."

"All the other salesmen had left and gone home; there was no one else here other than the cashier, the supervisor and myself."

"I'm sorry."

"I had to load up my car with bread and hot-cross buns. Did you know I live close to Grimshaw's shop; about half a mile away?"

"No I didn't. I don't know what to say."

"I mean, I am the managing director of this company, it's not my job to look after your customers. What exactly happened last Thursday morning?"

"Well, it all came about through him flatly refusing to give me his hot-cross bun order. He said he'd ordered plenty from the Scott's Bakery driver, and that he didn't need any from me."

"So, go on."

"Well, just like last Easter, he hadn't ordered enough. He'd run out of hot-cross buns an hour before I got there; which was exactly what happened last year, when he refused to give me an order then."

"Then why didn't you let him have some. You told the supervisor you had a few dozen to spare?"

"I did, and I would've let them have them if he and his wife hadn't spoken to me the way they did when I first walked into the shop. Ever since I started serving him he's done nothing but hurl abuse at Peter and I, for no reason at all – him and his wife."

"Well, maybe you should sit down for this." he said, his face breaking into a smile. "Would you like a cup of tea and a hot cross bun, I've got plenty in the boot of my car."

I was confused, wondering why he was smiling, wondering what he meant.

"Tell me, what did you think was going to happen to you today?"

"I wasn't sure what was going to happen. I've been worrying about it all weekend. I was hoping you'd understand why I did what I did. It was all on the spur of the moment. Like I said, I just lost it completely. I couldn't take it anymore. I'm just hoping you're not going to fire me. I'm trying to save up for a deposit on a house.

"Don't worry about that, I've no intentions of firing you."

"Thank you. So do I get my route back?"

"Yes, starting from tomorrow. By the way, you do know the Grimshaw's never did get their order, do you?"

"No, I didn't know. Why. I thought you said you took it over there yourself?"

“Because of the way he and his wife spoke to me, that’s why. I hardly got my foot in the door when they both started yelling, and shouting at me. I honestly don’t know how you’ve managed to put up with those two people for so long, I really don’t. In fact, my wife won’t even go in their shop for the same reason. She stopped going in the day that mini-market opened.”

“You mean I get to keep my job AND I don’t have to serve Grimshaw anymore?”

“Yes you get to keep your route and, NO, you don’t have to serve the Grimshaw’s anymore!”

“Wow, that’s a huge relief. Thank you!”

“He can get his bread from someone else in future. Maybe from that Scott’s salesman he kept going on to me about.”

“Did the supervisor tell you I sold Grimshaw’s bread and doughnuts to the mini-market further down the road?”

“Yes he did. In fact they rang this morning and placed a nice big order with us starting tomorrow. So you can go home and give your wife the good news and tell her you won’t have to deal with those awful people anymore.”

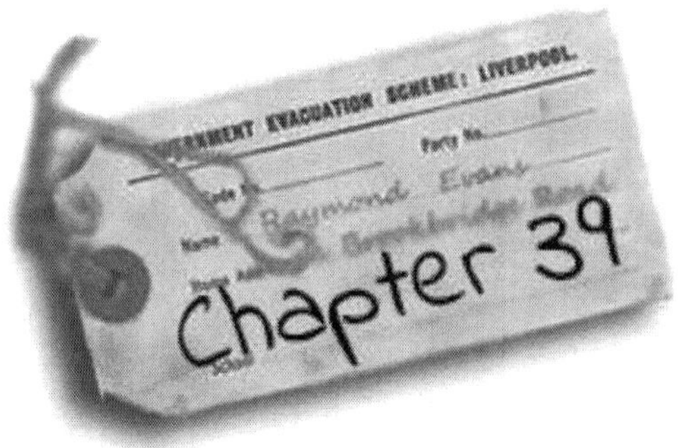

Harry's Sold Me A Heap!

It was 5.30 AM on a freezing cold and blustery morning when I was buzzing along Edge Lane keeping a close eye on the temperature gauge, watching it climb perilously close to the big red "H" on the dial.

Please God, please don't let it happen, not again, they'll give me the sack as sure as eggs are eggs if I'm late again.

God must have been busy elsewhere that morning because I only got as far as the traffic lights when the engine back-fired, bringing the car to an abrupt halt in the centre of the busy main road. I sat for a moment staring at the clouds of steam belching out from under the bonnet wondering what I should do next. I did think of unscrewing the radiator cap to release the pressure, but quickly changed my mind after remembering what happened last time I did that, when the radiator cap rocketed high up into the morning sky. So there I was, listening to the water bubbling away inside the radiator waiting patiently for the engine to cool down when this kindly person pulls up behind and not only helps push my car into a side street, but offers me a lift into work because he was going that way.

I was late by about twenty minutes that day, and all because of the heap of junk that scheming Harry Greenwood had sold to me. I couldn't afford to be late, not even by five minutes. It meant losing sales which of course meant losing lots of commission. Less money to put away towards a deposit on the house I was hoping to buy. Three times the car had broken down that week, once on my way to work and twice on my way home. Fortunately, one of the apprentice mechanics not only gave me a lift back to my car after I finished work that day, but he also got the engine running by patching up the water hose and cleaning up the oil drenched spark plugs.

> "You should ask Phil Armstrong to have a look at it," he said, "I wouldn't spend any more money on this car if I were you, not until he's had a good look at it."
>
> Why Phil Armstrong, why ask him? You know what he's like? He wouldn't help his grandmother across the road, even if she was in a wheelchair."
>
> "Yes, I know what you mean, but I'd seek his advice anyway if I were you. Maybe you'll catch him in one of his good moods. He's the best mechanic there. What Phil doesn't know about car engines isn't worth knowing."

The head mechanic Phil Armstrong knows all about cars and lorry engines - there's no doubt about that. Anyone who works for George Lunt's **will** tell you that. Just by putting his ear close to an engine, this man can figure out *exactly* what's wrong with your car. He can hear pings and clicking noises where other mechanics aren't able to. He knows all about manifolds, shock absorbers, struts and pistons, radiators, speedometers, etc, etc. Trouble is, he's a know-it-all, if you know what I mean. That's why no one likes him. Ask him one little question and he talks down to you like you were born without a brain; like he's the person that split the atom!

"I'll give you five minutes," Phil says, as he lifts up the bonnet. "That's all. Then I'm off home. I'm bloody sick of people coming up to me every few minutes asking me to look at their vehicles for 'nowt. There are other mechanics in this place besides me you know, or hadn't you noticed that!"

When he's finished listening to the engine, he takes out the dip-stick and slides it between his finger and thumb. Then after closely examining the miniscule drop of oil that's on the end of the dip-stick, he wipes it on his overalls and sticks it back inside the engine.

"Did you hear anything just then, Phil, any idea what the problem might be?"

"Give me a bloody chance, for God's sake. I haven't finished testing the thing have I? I need to drive it around the block. That's assuming this piece of junk will get me that far. Wait here 'till I get back. AND don't touch anythin'."

The car coughed, spluttered and backfired as he drove down the narrow cobblestone street leaving a thick cloud of black smoke in its wake.

"Get rid," he says, when he gets back.

"Get rid? You mean it's that bad? Is that what you're saying?"

"Worse. You've been done good and proper. It's on its way out. The engine's had it. I wouldn't spend another penny on it. I mean, just look at the amount of black smoke that was coming out of the exhaust when I drove off.

"It's really that bad, is that what you're trying to tell me?"

"Yes… and have you had any problems changing gear?"

"What do you mean?"

"Just doesn't feel right to me. It's like there's something loose inside. I could feel it every time I changed gear. It could be the selectors. But in plain English, your car's had it, mate. It's ka-put. Finito. It's had its day. You've been well and truly done!"

"Blimey."

"In fact, I wouldn't be surprised if someone's been messing around with the Odometer."

"The Odometer?"

"The mileage, I think it's been turned back."

"How do you know?"

"Just do, don't I? It's me job, isn't it?"

'Get rid'. Is that all he's got to say? I mean, he could have at least found a nicer way of putting it. Like, 'I'm sorry to pass on this bad news Ray, but I think it best if you change your car as soon as possible". That's all it takes. It won't cost him anything to be a little more pleasant - a little friendlier, especially when predicting the impending "death" of my little car.

"So going by what you've just told me, there's no telling how many thousands of miles this car's done?"

"That's right. Wouldn't surprise me if it's done double what it's showing on that clock. Who'd you buy it from?"

"Harry,"

"Who the hell's Harry?"

"Can't think of his last name right now, it's gone right out of my head."

"Are you tellin' me you can't remember the name of the bloke who sold you your car?"

"Hang on; it'll come to me in a minute. Faces I can remember, but names are always a problem."

"God almighty, fancy forgetting the name of whoever sold you this load of junk."

“He’s got long greasy hair and was a maintenance engineer here at one time. Now he sells second hand cars from home.”

“Long greasy hair?”

“Yes.”

“No idea who you’re talking about.”

“Talks very fast - always got a cigarette bobbing up and down between his lips.”

“Not Harry Greenwood?”

“Yes, that’s him, Harry Greenwood!”

“No wonder, I should have guessed. You’re going to have problems getting any money back from that shyster; he’s as bent as a butcher’s meat hook.”

“I won’t get any of my money back? But the car’s a wreck, you just said so yourself.”

“That won’t bother Harry, the deals done as far as he’s concerned. Scrooge is a spend thrift compared to that tight fisted conniving sod”.

“So that’s it then, I can’t do a thing about it?”

“You could go round to his house, I suppose, but I think you’ll be wasting your time.”

“I think I **will** go round to his house. I know where he lives.”

all I want is a peaceful world and a pork pie!

*****

Harry lives in a two up, two down terrace in one of the narrow back streets off Scotland Road, not far from the city centre. The very same house he was born in sixty something years ago. It's the only house in the street left standing, propped up at the sides with long metal supports. All the other houses have long gone; came under the big metal ball a couple of years after the war.

A small wrinkled hard of hearing old lady with frizzy white hair answers the door.

"Yes?"

"Is Harry in please?"

"Who?"

"HARRY."

"Arry! There's someone at the door asking for you."

"Who is it ma?"

"Someone's at the door to see you, son!"

"Yes I heard that ma, but who the hell is it?"

"What's your name luvvy?"

"RAY EVANS."

"Ray Evans, Arry."

"Jesus, what does he want now? Well take him into the parlor will you, ma?"

"Come in luvvy, 'ave a seat," his mother says, pointing to an old worn out couch, "He won't be long, he's just finishing his tea."

"Smells like he's having Kippers?"

"Sorry, didn't hear that luvvy, I'm a little deaf you see."

"I SAID IT SMELLS LIKE HE'S HAVING KIPPERS FOR HIS TEA!"

"Oh yes, 'Arry loves his kippers. Do you like kippers luvvy?"

"Yes I do, I love them."

"What?"

"I SAID YES, I LOVE KIPPERS."

"Oh you do? Would you like some then luvvy, we've got plenty?"

"No, no thanks, I'm..."

"What?"

"I SAID NO THANKS. I'M ON MY WAY HOME. MY WIFE WILL HAVE MY DINNER READY.

"Maybe a cup of tea and a buttered scone then, it won't take a minute?"

"No, but thanks all the same."

"What?"

"NO THANKS."

"They stink the house out don't they luvvy?"

"SCONES DO?"

"No silly, not scones, its kippers I'm talking about, they have that smell to them, don't they luvvy?"

By the time Harry enters the front parlor the conversation between his mother and me has reached a decibel level that would only be appropriate had I been speaking to her from another part of the city.

He stands in front of the fireplace rubbing his fat behind waiting for his mother to stop going on about her gallstones, lumbago and stiff joints. The miserly look on his face tells me he knows why I'm there.

"So, what can I do for yer lad," he says, interrupting his mother, "what's yer problem?"

"This car you sold me, it's a mess, there's all sorts wrong with it. It's always breaking down. I've had some problem or another every day since I bought it from you!"

"It was bought as seen," he says, "There's nothing I can do about that now. A deal's a deal."

"I need that car for work Harry; could you at least help me get it fixed to where it's reliable?"

Harry's face goes all pale and worried looking like I'm asking him to donate one of his kidneys.

"You must be joking, no I bloody well can't."

"But..."

"Nope!"

"But..."

"Nope! Not one penny!"

"But what about a spare wheel, it wasn't in the boot, and you said you'd see about getting me one. When are you going to do something about that?"

"Don't know what you're talking about a spare wheel. Anyway, like I said before, it was bought as seen. Now if you don't mind, I'm goin' back to my kippers."

"But I paid you good money for that car!"

"Bought as seen, nothing more to say, now are you going to leave or do I have to throw you out?"

I can see he's deadly serious, and given what Phil has told me earlier about him, decide I should call it a day and leave before I lose my temper and do something I might regret.

*****

"It's entirely my own fault," I told Lilian when I got home. "I feel so stupid for being so trusting. I should've asked around before I bought the car from him. It's a monumental disaster. I mean I've paid all that money out for a car that's absolutely worthless. A car that uses more oil than it does petrol and over-heats almost before I'm out of the driveway. And on top of all that, I've now been told by that sarcastic sod Phil Armstrong that I'm driving a vehicle that's done more miles than a rocket takes to get to the moon."

"Well what can we do about it? You need something reliable to get you to work."

"I'll have to get it fixed up so I can trade it in for something else, there's no other way. I can't sell it as it is. I'll get nothing for it."

"What about Chris Power, maybe he can help you get it running properly; he's very good with cars, isn't he? I'm sure he'll be a lot cheaper than taking it to a garage?"

That turned out to be a great idea of Lilian's. Chris agrees to come over to the house first thing Sunday morning to start working on the car. He tells me not to worry about the cost of the parts.

"I'll get 'used' parts for it, he says, "I'll buy them from a scrap yard I know over in Bootle. A mate of mine works there, he'll give me a good deal."

*****

Chris was able to replace the starter motor, spark plugs, fan belt, and a couple of rubber hoses all for just £4.00!

> "You are kidding? I said. "You sure that's all I owe you, just four quid?"
>
> "Yes," he says, "that's all the parts cost me. I bought them from that scrap yard in Bootle I told you about. I didn't see any point in buying new parts since you were planning to get rid of it."
>
> Later that afternoon, as I'm busy washing and polishing the car inside and out, getting it all spic and span in preparation for the trade-in, Phil Armstrong's voice pops into my head.
>
> ***'Someone's been tampering with this Odometer'*** I could almost hear him saying***, 'the mileage has been turned back'***.

I sat staring at the Odometer thinking how much easier it would be to sell the car with a much lower mileage on the clock. I grabbed a screwdriver and started working on the first screw, all the time ignoring the voice at the back of my mind warning me not to do it. The voice of reason finally prevailed just as I got to the last screw, my conscience getting the better of me. I immediately began screwing the Odometer back into place when I heard a sharp tapping noise on the window. It made me jump. It was Lilian standing there with a cup of tea in her hand. I reached over and opened the door.

"What are you doing? She said, handing me the cup of tea. "I hope you're not doing what I think you're doing."

"Well, I was, but I changed my mind."

"That's crazy Ray, you could get in some serious trouble doing something like that. Whose idea was that, Phil Armstrong's?"

"No, it was just a stupid idea that popped into my head. I'm not going to do it, see, I've put it back now."

"Well I'm glad you've changed your mind," she said, "You could have got yourself into all sorts of trouble. Anyway, why lower yourself to Harry Greenwood's level, that's the sort of thing he would do."

Just then she noticed a tiny piece of paper in the foot-well. She picked it up, and unfolded it.

"Where did this come from, who wrote this?"

"I don't know. It dropped out from behind the Odometer a few minutes ago. What does it say?"

"It just says, NOT AGAIN. What do you think it means?"

Thanks to Chris's mechanical skills and all his help, I did manage to get rid of the old car a lot quicker than I thought I would. We'd driven out to Southport for the day, and were about to head for home when I remembered my brother Frank telling me about a big car dealership nearby, the same dealership where he bought his car a few weeks earlier.

> “They’re the cheapest and largest car dealers in Southport” he’d said. “They’ve got a massive place out there and a huge selection of used cars to choose from. You can get any make you want; and none of them with a million miles on the clock. Only snag is, they’ve got these highly trained sales people, all trying their damnedest to force you into a deal right there and then. I can’t stand that sort of thing. But the cars are hard to beat. So if you do go there, be ready to stand your ground, don’t let them think you’re an easy mark.
>
> “Oh, and another thing, the sticker prices on the car windscreens – believe me, you can take them with a pinch of salt.”

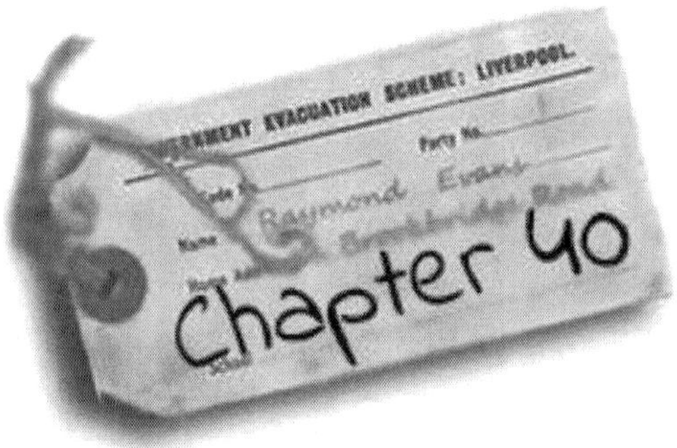

Southport's Slickest Salesman

I swung into the dealership parking area, switched off the engine and headed towards the used car section about a hundred yards from where I left Lilian sitting in the car with the baby. I was barely halfway across the tarmac when he came racing towards me, a big thick set man sporting a shiny double breasted suit with a tie he must have been wearing for a bet. The heavy gold chain around his wrist could have been bought in Woolworths.

"Good afternoon," he said, offering his hand, "what're you looking for today?"

"Saw your sign down the road, thought I'd drop in and have a look around, see what you've got to offer."

"I saw you getting out of that vehicle over there," he said, "Is **that** what you're looking to trade in?

"Yes... if I see anything I like, that is."

He marched straight over to the car, jumped behind the wheel, gave Lilian a quick nod and a fake smile and started up the engine.

"What year is it? Looks pretty old to me?"

"It's a 1950"

"Engine sounds a bit ropey, how much are you expecting to get for this?"

I don't like his bluntness, so I speak to him in the same manner he speaks to me. I mean, I am the customer after all.

"You tell me."

He shakes his head, blows a heavy sigh, steps out of the car and starts kicking the tires with the toes of his oxford brogues.

"What's the two bricks for?" he asks, as he opens up the boot, "Hand brake not working?"

The look on my face says it all. How the hell does he know about the hand brake not working?

"Don't worry," he says, "Don't get embarrassed. I've been in this business a long time. You need them for when you're parked on a steep hill, right? I know all the tricks."

"The brake cable's snapped; haven't had a chance to replace it."

"Right," he says, "I'll tell you what we'll do. Why don't you and the missus have a good look around while I see to that chap over there? I won't be long. Actually, before I go, we've a nice American car that might interest you," he says, pointing his finger, "can you see it? It's just a few cars along on your left. Go an' have a decco - I'll be back in a few minutes."

It was a 1950 Cadillac Sedan, half a street long with enough room for a football team. And it's while Lilian and I are looking over a black Vauxhall Victor next to the American car that Flash Harry creeps up from behind and taps me on the shoulder:

"Nice car, isn't it?" he says, "came in yesterday afternoon."

"I can't see any price." I tell him, nodding my head towards the windscreen, "How much is it?"

"One lady owner", he says, "that's all."

"How much are you asking for it?"

"Been garaged from the first day she bought it from us, when it was brand spanking new - actually it was me that sold it to her."

"How much do you want for the car?"

"Hundred and sixty to you," he says.

"Hundred and sixty?"

"Yep, and not a penny less."

"Can't you do any better than that?"

"Petrol consumption - thirty miles to the gallon."

"That's good to know, but how much are you willing to knock off?"

"Didn't say I was going to knock anything off the price, did I? Now where was I? Oh yes - top speed sixty miles per hour."

"Very nice, surely you can knock something off?"

"It's a family man's chariot that there car you're looking at. How much do you think it's worth?"

"Hundred and forty at the most."

"Hundred and forty? No way Jose. I'll give you forty quid for yours and take One Forty Nine for the Vauxhall, and that's my final offer."

"One forty nine? Er, let me think for a minute. How about..."

"There's no thinking about it. I've just told you; that's my last and final offer , one hundred and forty nine pounds Take - it - or - leave - it."

"I'll take it."

The shiny black Vauxhall Victor with its classy looking white-walled tyres and streamlined curves took my eye the moment I drove into the dealership. It wasn't a new car of course, but it was easy to see it had been well looked after by its one lady owner. Besides the soft leather seats and wood dashboard, what really took my fancy were the electronic traffic indicators. Instead of having to stick my arm out of a window when signaling a turn, all I needed to do now was simply flick a little switch. '*Bloody amazing, whatever will they think of next?*'

I was so taken up with the fancy traffic indicators that day that I decided to try them out on my way home by driving up and down a couple of side streets and back onto the main road again. What a mistake that was. I lost concentration on the last turn and finished up going in the wrong direction ending up a couple of miles out in the country on the wrong side of Southport.

"Lost your way again, have you?" Lilian asked, smiling to herself.

"Not really," I said, "just lost my bearings for a moment, that's all. I mean, I've been driving along this narrow winding country lane for God knows how long, for a good three or four miles if not more, and I haven't seen one solitary sign- post anywhere. It's a disgrace, that's what it is. I mean, even the bloody Romans had sign posts; right?"

"It's ok," she said, "I'm not complaining, we enjoy being driven around the countryside."

"Then what were you were smiling about just then, you must have been thinking of something to make you smile?"

"As a matter of fact I was. I was thinking about my mother, and what she's always saying about your driving."

"About my driving?"

"Yes, she's always telling me how much she enjoys riding in the car with you. In fact she was only talking about it just the other day while she was waiting for you to come home from work; waiting for you to drive her home."

"What's so funny about that? I know she likes riding in the car with me; she mentions it every time I drop her off."

"Yes, but I'll bet she hasn't told you the **real** reason why she likes riding in the car with you, has she?"

"Oh! And what reason might that be?"

"Well, she says she likes driving in the car with you because even though she's lived in Liverpool all her life, she sees parts of the city she never knew existed!"

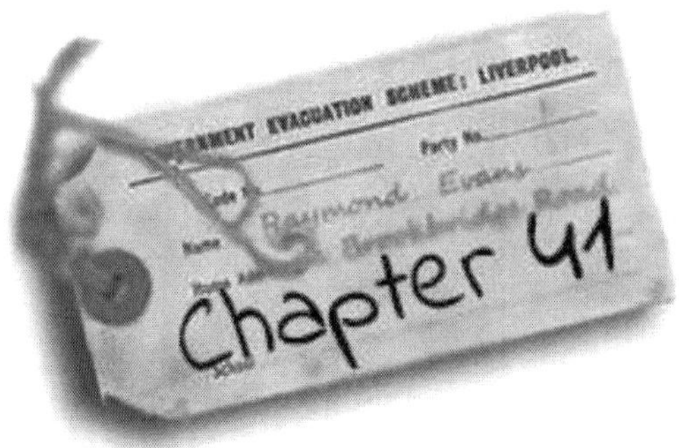

Saving In A Shoe Box

Dateline: One Sunday in June, 1961.

"It's a beautiful day out there, much too nice of a day to be stuck in the house. What do you think if we go for a run somewhere?"

Lilian agreed wholeheartedly and began getting the children ready once we'd finished lunch. Raymond was four, Debbie was a year old.

"Where are you thinking of going," she said; "have you got somewhere in mind?"

"Somewhere in the countryside," I said, "away from the city."

It wasn't long before we were heading out toward Whiston village, an area I'd become familiar with while searching for new stores to expand my latest delivery route for George Lunt's Bakery. Whiston then, was a fairly small semi-rural village, about ten miles or so outside Liverpool City limits.

I pull into windy Arbor Road and purposely slow down so Lilian can get a good view of the new bungalows they're starting to build.

"They look nice," I tell her, as I slow down and pull into the curb.

"Yes, they do look nice. Wonder what they're like inside?"

"I don't know," I tell her. "Why don't you go and have a look?"

"No, no, there's no point," she says, "I can see all I want to see from here."

"No point? We've got all day."

"I'd rather not," she says, "I'd rather wait until we can afford one"

"But you like looking at houses, just go and have a quick look; see what you think."

She turns back from the window.

"Is there something going on I don't know about?" she asks. "Why are you so interested in looking at new houses all of a sudden when we don't even have the deposit to put down on one?"

"Well, actually we ***DO*** have enough for the deposit."

"What do you mean, we have the deposit? Is this one of your jokes?"

“No. I've been putting a few pounds away each week for over a year now. I haven't told you because I wanted it to be a surprise. So, please, let's go and have a look."

"Hang on a minute, that's a LOT of money. Where exactly is this money?”

"I've got it hidden away in a shoe box."

"**Where**?"

"I'll tell you later. Let's go and have a look."

"So you knew about these houses all along; you've been here before?"

"Yes, last week.""I've got butterflies in my stomach. Are you serious? Can we really afford one of these bungalows? How much are they?"

"Two thousand two hundred pounds."

"How much a month?"

“About £11.00.”

“What about traveling to work? It's a long drive out here from Liverpool. Have you thought of that?”

"It's only about ten miles, but who cares, that's nothing when you look at how many miles I drive every day doing the bread route. It'll be worth the drive just to get away from the city."

"I've got butterflies in my stomach just thinking about it," she said. "Let's go and have a look at one."

We chose one of the four Bungalows that faced onto Windy Arbor Road. A tree lined thoroughfare that ran through the village past a group of shops, a red bricked Village Hall and pub called The Green Dragon.

"I just have a feeling this little house is going to bring us a lot of luck," Lilian said, when we moved in a few months later, "I'm sure it will."

How right she was.

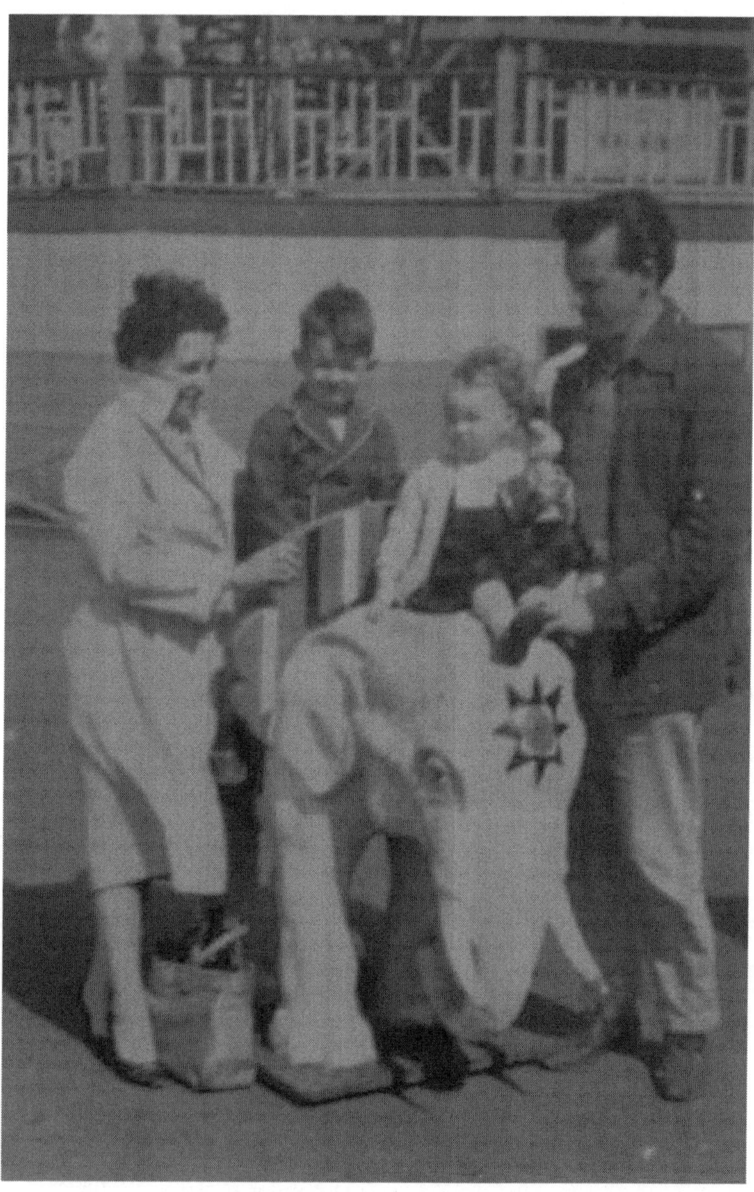

At Southport beach with Raymond & Debbie 1961-1962

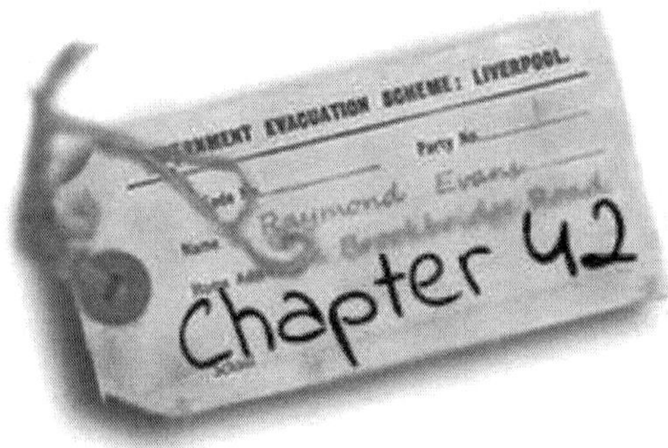

Springboard To Self-Employed

Dateline: Summer1965.

In those days I seemed to be on a never ending quest to find a way to move on and move up. I'd done very well at Lunt's and been, what I believe today they call 'head hunted' by a brand new state of the art bakery on the Huyton Industrial Estate, about a mile from the house. I began as a supervisor and worked my way up to area manager. A big part of my job was to find new areas to expand into; to build a sustainable delivery route before handing it over to a driver sales person.

I enjoyed the challenge of building new routes and the camaraderie among the twenty or so salesmen. I was making good money with a flat salary plus commission and a small over-ride on the salesmen, I was responsible for. But I still had a hankering to start up my own business so I could 'be my own boss' and finally be in control of my own destiny. Always on the look-out for ways to make a bit of extra money, I tried my hand at a number of "side-businesses" which included painting and decorating and selling carpets before establishing my calling in the clothing industry.

Princes Park Mansions, originally built for wealthy cotton barons and ship owners, had been renovated and re-configured as luxury apartments. I parked the car in the front of the building, raced up to the top floor apartment and rang the bell. I was greeted by a slender but matronly looking woman who I assumed to be 'Mrs.' Stewart, but later discovered she was his secretary come house keeper.

> "Sorry I'm a little late," I tell her, trying to catch my breath. "I have a six o'clock appointment with a Mr. Bryan Stewart. It's about the advertisement in the paper."

> "Come on through Mr. Evans," she says, "follow me."

Bryan Stewart, who's a dead ringer for the TV character Sergeant Bilko, rises from behind his desk to shake my hand.

> "Pleased to meet you Mr. Evans," he says, in a mild Scottish brogue, "take a seat."

> "Thank you. Sorry to have kept you waiting."

"It's no problem, I live here so it's not like I have to rush off to get home. Would you like something to drink, a cup of tea or something cool, a glass of orange juice maybe?"

"No thanks, I'm fine."

"Right then, let's get started. First of all, let me ask what you do for a living?"

"I'm area sales manager for a large bakery."

"You are? Oh, you have taken me by surprise. I'm looking for experienced salesmen with contacts in the retail clothing industry; I'm sorry but I thought I made that quite clear in the advertisement."

"Yes, I know, it did mention that."

"Do you have any connections in the retail clothing industry?"

"Well no, not really, not specifically in the clothing industry"

"Well in that case, if you don't mind my asking, Ray, why are you here?

"Your newspaper ad, it caught my attention."

"How was that then?"

I took the newspaper clipping out of my pocket and pointed to the advert.

"It was this part here where it says: 'There's no limit to what a good salesman can earn.' That's what brought me through your door today."

"I see," he says, removing his dark-rimmed glasses.

"But my company sells ladies outerwear – skirts, dresses, blouses and knitwear – not loaves of bread. Quite a big difference there don't you think?"

"That depends on how you look at it,"

"How do you mean?"

"At the end of the day it all comes down to how good a salesman you are doesn't it? As long as the product is good, it doesn't matter what you're selling, whether it's bread, cars ***or*** ladies clothing."

"And you class yourself as a good salesman, is that what you're saying."

"Yes, as long as I've got a good quality product to sell; one doesn't work without the other."

"Okay, that's fair comment, but you still need customers, and I only supply my salesmen with merchandise. I do not supply them with leads or customers, which regrettably you do not have."

"No I don't, but..."

"Well, let me ask you this, if you'd known about that, needing to supply your own customers, would you still have come here today?"

"Yes, I would! Having to supply my own customers doesn't bother me in the least. I think I've proven that with what I've done up to now."

"How so?"

"Well, with a business I started a few years ago and with the company I'm with now. They approached me when they opened their brand new bakery. They brought me in to help them get started. The bread business is very cut throat and very competitive."

"I see, but what was this other business you mentioned, what was that?"

"Hiring out washing machines."

"Come again, I'm not sure I'm with you."

"I bought four washing machines and hired them out by the hour."

"Hiring washing machines? I'm not sure if I'm following you correctly"

"I hired out washing machines to people who couldn't afford a washing machine of their own; who normally did their weekly wash in the kitchen sink, or at the wash house, just like my mother did."

"Well now, that **is** interesting. I've never heard of anything like that before. How'd you get that started?"

"I went around in the evenings after work knocking on doors to get customers singed up. Once I was satisfied I had the right amount, I went and bought the machines on hire-purchase."

"I see. So what happened to your little washing machine rental business then?

"I sold it. The machines were beginning to break. I should have bought commercial machines and not the household type. They weren't designed to be used 50-60 times a week, the motors weren't strong enough, that's why they were starting to burn out, why I had to replace them. Fortunately, someone had already asked me about buying the business, so I decided to sell it to him and look for something else.

"So now you're area sales manager for a large wholesale bakery business?"

"Yes."

"Do you have a company car?"

"Yes."

"Petrol allowance?"

"Yes."

"So it seems like you've done very well for yourself since you've been there?"

"Yes."

"Do you own your own home?"

"Yes. Why would you want to know that?"

"Because I'm not sure why you're here? I mean, that's a good job you have right now, you're making good money. It sounds like it's pretty secure, why give it all up?"

"I'm here because I'm looking to move on. I don't want to be a bread salesman all my life. I want to make a better life for my family, and to my mind the only way to do that, is to be my own boss. That's the only way I'll ever have control over the future - my own income."

"Well I can understand where you're coming from, but you have to realize, I need people who know the clothing business inside out, people who've been in the rag-trade (as we call it) for a long time. This is a competitive business too, Ray. That's why I'm looking for people with lots of contacts, who can move large quantities. It's imperative I keep the stock turning over, otherwise I'm in big trouble. That's how this business works."

"Mr. Stewart, your ad really caught my attention, where it said *'there's no limit to what a good salesman can earn.'* I know I'm a good salesman. I'm just looking for a chance to put that to the test.

"So you think this could be the opportunity you've been looking for?"

"Yes, I think it's exactly the kind of opportunity I've been looking for!"

"Well Ray, you seem pretty keen and that's half the battle right there. I still have concerns about you being able to find new customers though. I don't want you poaching customers from my regular salesmen"

"I won't do that. I give you my word I won't. If you just let me know where to stay away from, I'll go and find my own without causing you any problems with your other sales people. I do have just one question though. Is this position commission only or do you pay a basic salary as well?"

"Neither."

"Neither? I don't understand?"

"The salesmen here work for themselves Ray. They are wholesalers in their own right. They don't work for me, they're self employed. I'm just their supplier."

"So in other words, they buy the garments from you and then add on their own profit?"

"Yes, each sample, (which I'll show you in a second) has a price tag showing the price I want for that particular garment. That's how it works here. But, with all due respect, there is no way someone without the proper contacts can sell this type of merchandise, especially in the quantities I'm talking about. Let me show you what I mean."

He took me along the hall to his sample room. And although I knew very little about the ladies' fashion trade at the time, even

I could see his garments were of the highest quality. I went along the rails getting a closer look at the price tags, mentally calculating what I thought that particular item might retail for. And even as green as I was, I knew, without a shadow of a doubt the margin would leave me more than enough room for a very satisfactory profit.

I asked him if he wouldn't mind selling me one of the jumpers for my wife. He pointed to the rails and told me to help myself. I picked a lilac one in Lilian's size. I wanted to get her opinion on this stuff, just in case I **was** missing something. The prices of two pounds seemed so ridiculously low considering the quality.

> "Ray," he said, shaking my hand, "you seem like a decent bloke, but I'm sorry to say, with no knowledge of the rag trade, I just don't think it'll work. It's been nice meeting you and I thank you for coming. All the best"

And with that, I was back out in the parking lot with nothing more than a great deal on a jumper. Then again, my head was spinning.

*****

> "Surely this can't be the price he's charging his salesmen?" Lilian asked.
>
> "Yes it is," I said, "that is the price."
>
> "But its Merino Wool," she said, "It couldn't possibly be

manufactured for this price – even I know that, and I'm not in the manufacturing business. What else does he sell besides jumpers?"

"Skirts, dresses, and blouses."

"It can't be right," she said. There's something very fishy about this whole set-up, if you ask me."

I could see where her mind was going, down the very same road mine had.

"That's what I thought at first. But you'd need to see his set-up. It's all very professional and above board. I mean he **doesn't** come across as a dodgy type of person."

"Well if they were stolen, I doubt he'd be advertising for salesmen in the paper, and interviewing them in his fancy flat in Princes Park Mansions! He'd probably have his stuff hidden in a lock-up down some back alley."

"Okay, let's suppose he **IS** legit, you're not thinking of working for him are you? It's a crazy idea if you are. Like he said, you don't know anything about the clothing business. It'll never work. You don't have the contacts."

"I was thinking about that on the way home and I think I may have come up with the answer to that."

"Go on."

"As far as I know, his salesmen sell only to the retail trade."

"So? What does that mean?"

"Well, after seeing his prices and the quality of his merchandise, I think there's more than enough room left over to interest a wholesaler, or a few wholesalers, come to that."

"Surely his salesmen have thought of that? There must be a reason they haven't done so before now."

"I know. I thought about that too. My guess is they haven't because of their greed. They'd rather sell to retailers and make a bigger profit for themselves.

"So you're thinking of giving up your nice safe, secure job to become a wholesaler?"

"No, no… well, not right away, that'd be far too risky. But I wouldn't mind giving this rag trade a try – on the side I mean; just to see how I get on. All I need to do is find myself a few wholesalers."

"But how are you going to do that?"

"Knock on their doors and show them a sample, what's simpler than that?"

"What did Bryan Stewart say about that idea?"

"Nothing. Like I said, I didn't think of it until I was on my way home. But you know what, it doesn't matter. I wouldn't be working for him, would I? I'd be working for myself. All he cares about is moving large quantities, every week. That sounds like wholesale to me!"

"Well I should've guessed there was *something* going on inside your head, otherwise, why bring this jumper home for me to look at?"

"Because I wanted your opinion on it; I wanted to know what you thought of the quality and the crazy price he was asking for it. And it **IS** a crazy price, you've already confirmed that yourself. I'll go see him after work tomorrow."

*****

I called Bryan Stewart the next day and managed to talk him into giving me a few minutes of his time. He said he could see me around six. Not wanting him to see me as a bread salesman, I rushed home, threw off my work clothes, and changed into a suit.

"But you know nothing about the clothing industry, Ray. I'm sorry, but it just will not work. And anyway, what about your job? You've got a young family to think of, you'd be crazy to give up the security. I've already told you that."

"Just a couple of weeks, that's all I need."

"Two weeks?

"Yes. I'll take two weeks off work. I'm due some holiday time anyway, but I'll go sick if I have to."

"To do what?"

"To find a wholesaler interested in this stock you want to move quickly. I'm sure I can do it. In fact I know I can. All I need is a sample, and I'll be on my way."

"And where are you thinking of going with this sample?"

"Scotland, none of your salesmen go up there, so I won't be poaching anyone's customers."

"How do you know that?"

"You told me the other day in the interview. You said you were hoping to take on a couple of salesmen living in or near Edinburgh. Please - just give me a chance, that's all I ask. You've got nothing to lose, right? "

I could feel him starting to break. In fact I think I got him with that last question, which after all was very true – he had nothing to lose and everything to gain. But then so did I.

"Okay" he said, sounding almost too tired to argue anymore. "You've won me over. When can you start?"

"Next week. I'll need to organize the time off from work, but it won't be a problem, I'll get it sorted."

"Right then," he said, "why don't you take four samples of the skirt I've already shown you, (one of each colour and size) and let's see how you go on with them."

"How many do you want me to sell?"

"Well, I'd be **really** impressed if you could move the whole lot - three thousand pieces, cash on delivery. That would make me a very, very happy person."

“How much?”

“Two quid.”

“Two quid it is then. Thanks Bryan, I can’t wait to get started.”

“Don’t get too excited, Ray, this is a hard game, it’s not like selling loaves of bread.”

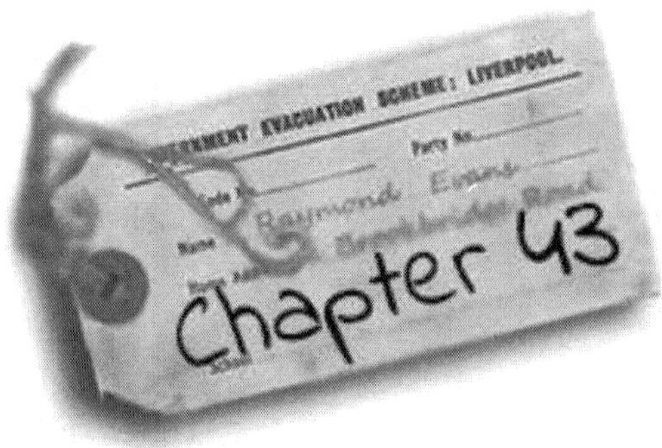

Selling Skirts To A Scot

It's Monday morning, the first day of my two weeks holiday. I've made three phone calls so far and got absolutely nowhere. The first one told me to call back tomorrow. The second (without even asking about prices) said he's got skirts coming out of his ears, and the third, (contradicting what his advert in the yellow pages said) told me he doesn't even sell ladies fashions. '*What's that all about?*'

Regardless, *I mustn't give up,* I told myself. *Let's see what this next fella has to say for himself.* I managed to breeze by the receptionist, which was a nice surprise.

"Hello, McBride Wholesalers, can I help you?"

"Yes. Can I speak to Mr. McBride please?"

"Yes, who can I say is calling?"

"Ray Evans."

"Just a moment Mr. Evans, I'll get him for you."

"Hello, McBride speakin"

"Hello Mr. McBride, Ray Evans here. I'm calling to see if you might be interested in looking at a ladies skirt sample?"

"Might be, where ya callin from laddie?"

"Liverpool."

"And what's the name of the company?"

"R & L Fashions." I said, almost panicked

"R & L Fashions? Never heard of it."

"That's because we've not done business up in your area before, Mr. McBride?"

"Oh is that so, and how'd ye find out about us?"

"Looked you up in the Yellow Pages."

"I see, and what have ye got to show me agin?"

"A ladies classic, pure wool, fully lined skirt, that I'm sure you'll be very interested in."

"And ye 're comin' all the way up here from Liverpool with just the one sample; that's a wee bit of a chance ye takin' isn't it?

"My boss doesn't want them sold down here in Liverpool, that's the reason I'm coming up there with them."

Yer gonna be a wee disappointed if ah dinna like it, cumin all the way up here?"

"I'm pretty confident you will like it."

"What if ah dinna like the price yer askin'?"

"I don't think that'll happen either, Mr. McBride. But then, on the other hand if you don't like the skirt or the price, that'll be fine too. As I said, I'm going to be up in your area anyway. I'll be calling on a couple of other wholesalers just a bit further up from you in Edinburgh. Oh, and another thing Mr. McBride while we're talking, because there's three thousand of these high quality skirts, I'm not able to offer you any credit, it'd have to be cash on delivery"

"Three thousand, yer say? Auch, that's nuthin' laddie, yer dinna have to worry about that. We're the biggest buyers of Ladies clothin' around these parts, probably in all o' Scotland. By the way, why doesn't your boss want them sold in Liverpool, we're not dealin' in stolen goods here, are we?"

"Stolen goods? No, no nothing like that Mr. McBride. It's all quite genuine; you'll have a full invoice and an exclusive in Scotland as long as you take them all."

"Suit ye'self then, what time are yer thinkin' ye'll be here?"

"I should be there around twelve'ish, will that work for you?"

"Aye, I'm here all day tomorra'. I'll be expecting ye at twelve then."

"Right, thanks I'll see you tomorrow."

"Fine laddie, I'll pass yer back to ma secretary, she'll give ye the directions – 'bye!"

*****

It's around mid-day when I pull into Langholm – a small picturesque town situated deep in the heart of Dumfriesshire. I pull over to the side of the road to double check the directions.

Follow the road over the stone bridge, until you come to a bend in the road, past the church on your right. About 100 yards or so, you'll see the warehouse on the right.

I've just rounded the bend when the warehouse comes into view. A large painted sign over the delivery dock confirms I've arrived at J. McBride, Wholesaler of Quality Ladies Clothing. Negative thoughts suddenly start flying around inside my head.

What if he doesn't like the skirts?

What if he thinks the price is too high?

What if he's just giving me the run around?

I can almost hear him saying 'nah laddie, they're not what I was expectin', sorry.'

"Mr. McBride is expecting you, Mr. Evans," the receptionist says. "His office is the first door on your right down the hall, just give him a knock."

Jimmy McBride, a smart slim forty year old opens his office door and invites me in.

"Sorry I'm a little late Mr. McBride, took the wrong turning off the A7."

"Dinna matter," he says, shaking my hand,

"Would ye like a cuppa tea, there's a fresh pot just made?"

"No thanks, I had one when I stopped for breakfast"

Thinking back, (because I was nervous inside; because there was a lot riding on the meeting) I refused the tea in case he saw my hands shaking while holding the cup.

After examining each of the four skirts as if he were authenticating a rare masterpiece painting, he picked up the phone and called his secretary in from the adjoining office.

"Please lass," he said, handing her one of the skirts, "if yer dinna mind."

She takes the skirt from him and disappears back into her office.

"Second opinion," he said, twisting around in his swivel chair, "always best ta have a second opinion."

I nodded in agreement.

“She’s damn good ye ken... Ah never buy anythin' without her approval. If she dinna like it, I dinna buy it.”

“How long has she been with you?”

“Twenty long years” his wife says jokingly as she enters the office.

“Well, what de ye think lass,” Jimmy asks.

“Very nice,” she says, giving a twirl in the middle of his office, “fits perfectly. I like it a lot. What are they costing us?”

“Two pounds ten shillings,” he says, turning to face me, “that’s what ye want for em, right Ray?”

“Yes, that’s right.”

“Full size range, did ye say?”

“Yes, sizes tens through eighteens.”

“Even breakdown over the four colours as well as two skirt lengths?”

“Yes.”

“All perfect garments, all of ‘em, right? No seconds? You’re absolutely sure about that, Ray?

“Yes.”

“Which will be clearly stated on ya invoice, that all 3000 skirts are perfect garments?”

"Yes, that's correct."

"Any movement on the price if ah take em all?"

"No sorry, none whatsoever.I don't believe in jacking the price up just to bring it back down again."

"Auch, come on Ray, yer can do better than that. Do ye have any idea what they were retailin' for in the stores?"

"I don't think there's any left in the stores right now, as far as I know. But I do know they were selling for fourteen ninety nine or fifteen ninety nine, depending on the size."

"Ok, yev got yourself' a deal," he says, offering his hand like he really means it this time. "Now then, when can ye get them here?"

"Tomorrow suit you, around mid-day?

"That'll suit me fine; and if ye dinna mind, I'll keep these four samples, just add em onto the invoice tomorrow."

"Yes, sure, no problem."

"Aye, well that's that then, see ye ta'morra!"

I left Jimmy's warehouse and stopped at the first phone box to pass on the good news to Bryan.

"How did you get on," his secretary asks, "Did you manage to sell them? Mr. Stewart's not here right now, he won't be back until tomorrow."

"Yes, I sold them all, the whole three thousand!"

"Oh my, that's wonderful news, I'm so pleased for you Ray" she says, "and he'll be so pleased as well. I'll give him the message as soon as I can get hold of him. He's been waiting all morning to hear from you."

"Freda, would you please have the order counted and loaded into your van ready for me to leave no later than seven o'clock tomorrow morning."

"Yes, of course," she says, "Don't worry, I'll call the warehouse and make sure they have everything ready for you."

I called Lilian and told her the good news too.

*****

It's just turning six thirty in the morning when I arrive at the warehouse. Charlie, the warehouse manager is loading the last of the skirts into the van.

"Bryan wants you to show your customer these samples" Freda says, handing me three Merino Wool lady's jumpers. "He's desperate to move them."

"How many are there?"

"Four thousand," she says, "what do think, do you think you can sell these as well?"

"How much does he want for them?"

"I don't know," she says, handing me an envelope, "he didn't say. All the details are inside the envelope. Oh and by the way, he'd like Charlie to go along with you. Hope you understand."

"Yes, of course, no problem."

******

It's just turning eleven thirty as I swing into McBride's yard and follow the 'Goods Inward' sign to a loading dock, at the rear of the warehouse. A young girl unlocks the door and after checking who I am, hands me an envelope.

"It's from Mr. McBride," she says, "he said I've not to accept the skirts from ye"

My mind starts spinning trying to take in what she's just said. What's she talking about. What's going on?

"Sorry, come again, what did you just say?"

"It's all in the note," she says, "sorry, but I've got customers to see to."

"Hey! Where are you going," I shout, but it's already too late. I bang my fist on the door, "come back here, what's the hell's going on? He ordered these skirts just yesterday!"

I turned around and started back toward the van when I heard the door open behind again

"I'm sorry, Mr. Evans," she says, "but I've no idea what's going on. I'm just a student. I only work here part time and all I know is what he told me: "Whatever you do don't let him unload the skirts!"

"I'm totally confused, where **is** Mr. McBride?"

"Sorry, but I've no idea where he is." she said, before disappearing back inside the warehouse.

I rip open the envelope about to read the note when Jimmy's car pulls into the yard.

"See yer got ma note," he shouts sounding entirely too cheery for my taste at this point.

I remind myself to hold my temper and also that Charlie is watching all of this from the van. I don't want him going back to his boss telling him I have no idea what I'm doing.

"What the heck's going on Jimmy? I don't understand. I've just been told you've changed your mind about the skirts?"

"Changed ma mind about what? He shouts from his car."

"She just told me you don't want the skirts."

"Auch, that'll be ma daughter, sorry about that, she's got mixed up with somethin' else. She just helps out when we're busy"

"So you've not changed your mind?"

"Nay laddie, it's all there in the note. I **TOLD** her ta tell ye ta read the note. Did she not tell ya?"

I looked down at the note:

Ray,

Do not off-load the skirts, leave them in the van until I get back. I don't want the customers seeing them yet. I'm going to have them stored in another warehouse. I want to get rid of the skirts I've already got before they see these. I've gone to the bank to get your money. Grab yourself a cup of tea, I'll be right back.

Jimmy.

"No, no laddie, I hav'na changed ma mind. Dinna ken where the young lassie's got that one from. Must've overheard somethin' in ma office – aye, that's what'll it be. She's just got the wrong end of the stick ah think she has."

By this time it's starting to sink in that he does want the skirts. That it's all a misunderstanding. My stomach still thinks otherwise though, as I watch Jimmy nonchalantly hop up into the back of the van and grab a cellophane pack of skirts off the rail.

"There's two hundred and fifty packs hung up in there Jimmy, twelve in a pack, three thousand skirts in total."

"Aye, and all in size and colour ratio I see, very nice indeed. Well done laddie; nice doin' business with ye!"

"Oh, by the way, I've got three beautiful lady's Merino Wool jumpers in the cab to show you as well, wanna see them?"

"Sure," he said, "I'll take a look at them in the office while the lads off-load the skirts in ma other warehouse"

We head into the office to exchange the invoice and payment. His wife comes through to look at the samples.

"Oh they're beautiful," she says, holding one against her, "I've got to have one of these."

"Ah have 'na bought 'em yet; depends how much he's askin'."

"Two pounds ten shillings," I tell him, handing him the note with a full breakdown of the colors and sizes.

"How many?"

"Four thousand, all perfects."

"I'll take the lot," he says, without a hint of hesitation, "Cash on delivery. When can ah have em?"

I wonder am I dreaming this or what? I ask myself. Is this REALLY happening to me?

"Will tomorrow suit you, about the same time?"

"Suits me just fine," he says, "ye money'll be wait'n fer yer laddie."

all I want is a peaceful world and a pork pie!

The profit from those two deals allowed me to take the first steps toward finally starting my own wholesale clothing business. It was a business I learned by trial and error as I grew into it. Lilian and I worked together side by side for the next 34 years until we finally sold up and retired to America, but that's another story…

Profit on the two deals....

3000 skirts @ 10 shillings a skirt = £1,500.

4000 jumpers @ 10 shillings a jumper = £2,000.

Total profit - £3,500.

Over a thousand pounds more than we paid for our first home!

*****

Meet ‘n Greet , VIP Readers & Book Signings:

Ray is available to meet with book clubs, reading groups, schools and academic institutions in person based on location or via Skype and video conferencing through his VIP Reader Program.

Book signings and fund raising events typically incorporate our exclusive narrated video covering a brief background explanation about Britain during WWII and Operation Pied Piper. This is typically followed by a Q&A discussion of how Ray’s early life experiences shaped him and his life as an adult.

Contact us at:

RayEvansAuthor.com/Contact

all I want is a peaceful world and a pork pie!

Connect With Ray:

Follow Ray on Twitter:

@RayEvansAuthor

Facebook:

Facebook.com/RayEvansAuthor

Author Blog:

RayEvansAuthor.com

Author Bio

Born in Liverpool, England in 1933 into a family of 7, Ray Evans was evacuated to the South Wales town of Llanelli at the outbreak of World War Two. He remained there until the cessation of hostilities in 1945, when he and his family were returned to Liverpool to re-build their family and their lives.

Despite his initial dislike of being in South Wales and Llanelli, he grew to love the beautiful Welsh countryside and learned firsthand of the love and genuine warmth of the Welsh people. Now feeling like a duck out of water yet again, but yearning for the gently rolling hills and green valleys of South Wales, Ray vowed he would move out of the city as soon as he possibly could.

When he left school Ray worked first at the State Restaurant in Liverpool as a cooks apprentice and then for Hanson's Dairy as a delivery man before going into the Army to complete his two years National Service as a member of the Royal Army Medical Corps in Egypt.

He returned to Liverpool and in 1956 married his wife Lilian and shortly thereafter moved out of the city limits to the small village of Whiston. Lilian and Ray have one son and a daughter. In 1964 Ray started a wholesale clothing business and he and Lilian ran this enterprise together highly successfully until 1995, when they moved to the USA to be closer to their daughter and granddaughter (the inspiration for his writing the book).

Shortly after moving there Ray began writing the book at the suggestion of his daughter and with the encouragement of Lilian to help ensure the stories would be passed on to all of their grandchildren and generations to come.

In 2001 the family moved once more and settled in the gentle rolling hills and green fields near Williamsburg, Virginia, which with all its history and connections to England feels just like home. The first edition of Before the Last All Clear was published in 2005, with a second edition released to the American market in August 2008, being published on Kindle in 2011.

The most common question Ray was asked at book signings and events was, “what happened after the war?” That’s what inspired him to write the next part of his memoir “All I Want Is A Peaceful World…& A Pork Pie!”

In the process of writing the books, Ray came to realise more than ever before, how the importance of having a home had impacted his life during the evacuation and far beyond. He supports many related charities by actively participating in fund raising events.

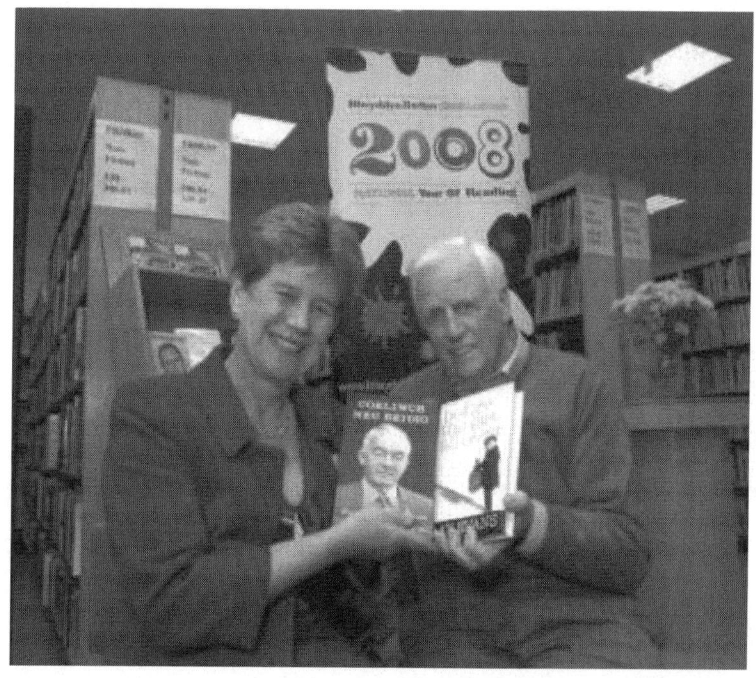

Before The Last All Clear was voted

#1 Readers Choice

2008 Welsh Books Council Year of Reading
(English Language Selection)

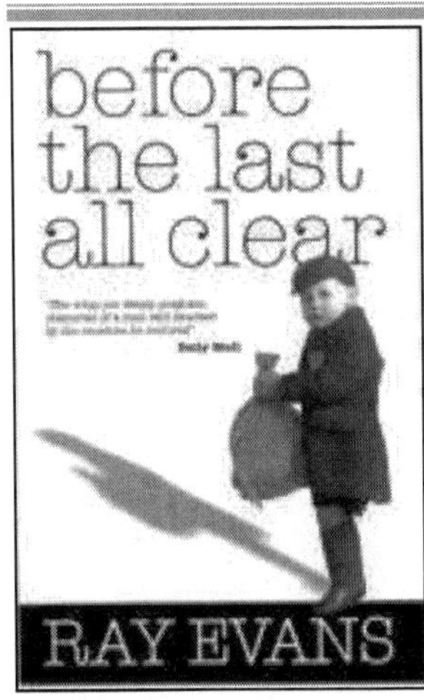

Other books by Ray Evans

Synopsis

During World War II around three and a half million British people were evacuated away from possible air raids in the big cities in one of the largest social upheavals Great Britain has ever seen. The Government evacuation program was named Operation Pied Piper.

Many of the evacuees were children. Journeys from the cities were long and tiring and the evacuees did not know where they were going. They were often dropped off in groups and gathered in a local village hall or school to be 'chosen' by the prospective foster parents. One of those children was Ray Evans whose family was transported from Liverpool to a small town in Wales called Llanelli.

In "Before the Last All Clear", Evans tells a harrowing tale of leaving his mother and being forced to live with families who at best regarded him as a nuisance and, at worst, exploited him.

Evans' account takes a happy turn when he is billeted to a family who make him so welcome that he is reluctant to leave them at the end of the war.

Written in a simple, direct style "Before the Last All Clear" depicts a world far removed from the glamour and sophistication of the twenty-first century.

all I want is a peaceful world and a pork pie!

Watch video trailers and learn about Ray's VIP Reader programs for schools, colleges, reading groups, book clubs and fund raising events for charities at:

BeforeTheLastAllClear.com

RayEvansAuthor.com

Professional Reviews:

A touching memoir of a child's experience as a World War II evacuee in England. At the age of six, Evans, along with thousands of other British children, was separated from his family, home and school and sent to the safety of the English countryside during WWII. In his memoir, the author recalls the emotions of a small child who misses his mother and family. While it may be easy for readers to become emotional when it comes to this kind of story, Evan's touching account is indeed a tearjerker; he aptly recaptures his fear and the feeling of being lost as he made his way to his temporary home. He presents a tale of horror as he relives the memories of two homes where he stayed during the evacuation period. As a castoff evacuee, Evans was often mistreated by the families with whom he stayed, enduring what Western society today would consider child abuse. By the time the author reaches his third and final home, he loves it so much that he almost doesn't want to leave. Evans' illustrative writing capably paints each scene, making it easy to imagine the conditions in which he lived. In fact, it would be realistic to picture this cute young boy's life portrayed on screen. *Before the Last All Clear* is a well-written account of a lovable protagonist who yearns for a sense of normalcy—all while remaining optimistic that the war will soon end and better days are ahead.

A beautiful memoir of WWII as seen through the eyes of a child.

Kirkus Discoveries, Nielsen Business Media, 770 Broadway, New York, NY 10003

all I want is a peaceful world and a pork pie!

Reviewed by:Rod Clark BEFORE THE LAST ALL CLEAR - Author Ray Evans.

Anyone who has shared a cup of tea or two with English people who lived through the bombing of England and Wales during World War II knows how deeply those terrible events shaped their lives and scarred their memories. In wartime large numbers of children were moved from heavily bombed areas (particularly in places like London and Liverpool) to billet homes in other parts of Great Britain that were deemed safer from the German bombs. Regrettably, the billeting system, both in Great Britain (and in Canada) was often flawed, and those weaknesses were aggravated by the shortages and ravages of war. Before the Last All Clear is the poignant and disturbing memoir of a young evacuee from Liverpool, Ray Evans, who as a young boy was billeted in Wales during the worst of the war years, and suffered there under very difficult circumstances. Of the six homes Ray lived in, three were horrific, and three provided happier memories. In sometimes painful detail, but with a healthy dose of dark humor, Mr. Evans' memoir gives the reader an unforgettable look at War time Britain and Wales as seen through the eyes of a child. With him we huddle in flimsy shelters as the German bombers thunder overhead. We feel his hunger as his rations are stolen to feed other children in the families with which he is billeted, and he is forced to steal food.How he is locked in a closet for hours for sins he did not commit. How he is twice infected with scabies while living in the billets, and is twice horrendously cured. We share his joy as he earns three pennies on a cider run and goes to the cinema to see Popeye and Gene Autry. We laugh incredulously as we hear how he takes a live German bomb to the local police station and plunks it on the counter in front of the terrified constabulary. We hear his crusty grandfather explain why he made tea and toast in the kitchen during a bombing raid instead of hiding in the cellar: "If Adolph f*&#$%g Hitler wants me dead, he'll have to come over to England and shoot me himself!" All in all, this is a superb portrait of wartime Britain seen from a child's perspective, and recalled in astounding and excruciating detail by a man who lived through it and tells all. Before the Last All Clear is a superb memoir, but more importantly, it is a vivid and uniquely personal morsel of history that any reader will find difficult to forget.

www.beforethelastallclear.com

all I want is a peaceful world and a pork pie!

Glossary:

This is a very brief alphabetical list of non-technical explanations for some of the slang terms and typically British names for things that are referred to throughout the book.

Back the fire up = Typically adding more coal and then a layer of slack (fine coal dust) on top to slow the burn rate.

Bonnet = Hood of a car.

Bungalow = Single story home, some had “dormers” to allow for bedrooms to be built into what would otherwise have been attic space.

Car boot = Trunk

Chemist = Pharmacy.

Cheque = Check

Chippy = Fish & Chip Shop

Clothing Coupons = When you went to buy clothes you not only needed the money but also to have the ration coupons to allow you to buy.

Cock-eyed = Slang meaning not straight.

Crisps = Potato Chips

Cumberland Sausage = Traditional regional savory sausage from northern England

Decco = Liverpool slang for “take a look”

Dual Carriageway = Two lane or divided highway

English clothing sizes = US typically two sizes smaller so a UK 10 is a US 8

Flats = British name for purpose built multi-family apartment type buildings

Fortnight = Fourteen days

Half-Crown = Coin (unit of money)

Hire Purchase = Buying on credit

Jumper = Sweater

L-Plates = Standardized sign required to be clearly displayed on vehicles when anyone who is not fully licensed yet is driving. The sign is a white square with a large red capital L - to make it clear and advise other drivers you lack driving experience.

Lift = Elevator

Lino = Linoleum flooring

Lorry = Large delivery truck.

Nikki Lauder = Famous Formula One race car driver.

Nowt = British slang meaning nothing

Old Blighty = Common nickname for England

Petrol = Gas

Pips = Gold bars on a uniform defining rank

Pram = Old fashioned baby stroller it's proper full name being "perambulator"

Pre-fab = Prefabricated homes similar to (but much more simple than) today's manufactured homes

Pub = Licensed public house, local bar

Ration Books = Many things were rationed during WWII and for a number of years afterwards. Food, Clothing, Gasoline among them.

Robin Reliant = Three Wheeled Motor Vehicle, the butt of many jokes in the UK

Seconds (Clothing) = Irregular or slightly imperfect garments are often referred to as "seconds" meaning second grade or second quality. Imperfections could be extremely small and an entire business developed out of large companies using minor defects as an excuse to reject an order leaving manufacturers with no option but to sell the goods at a reduced price. As time went by the large chain stores began putting more and more restrictions on how the manufacturers could sell rejected goods. The manufacturers made so much on the orders they did fulfill that it was still very attractive for them to work with chain stores. However an entire "seconds" industry developed around this practice during the early sixties and is still prevalent in the UK today.

Shilling, Sixpence and Pennies = Units of money, coins

Skirting Board = Baseboard

Skiving = Lazy, avoiding work

Slack = Fine coal dust, helped to slow down the burn rate and kept a fire more likely to stay lit for longer.

Taking the Mickey = Making fun of

Tallyman = Door to door catalogue salesman, often sold on credit

Tea cozy = Thermal cover for tea pot

Ten Bob Note = Paper money – Value ten shillings

Thick = English slang term meaning "not too bright or quick to catch on to things".

"V" sign = When issued with the back of the hand facing away, is the equivalent of "flipping the bird". When issued with the front of the hand facing away is a victory sign

Washing = Laundry

Wazzock = English slang for idiot

British Monetary System

One last thing that probably requires explanation especially for anyone who didn't grow up in the UK before the "other D-Day". British money today is based on a decimal system where 100 pennies equals one pound, it's a very simple and straight forward system, that was actually only introduced on 15th February 1971.

Prior to that the British (pre-decimalisation) system of coinage was introduced by King Henry II (Henry was a Plantagenet – essentially meaning he was 'mostly' French even though he was King of England at the time) around 1158, although he continued to 'tweak' the system and the coins, through about 1180.

Anyway what's important to know, is that the system was based on the troy weight of precious metals. So the 'penny' was literally one 'pennyweight' of silver. A pound sterling weighed in at 240 pennyweights, or a 'pound of sterling silver'.

The symbols '**s**' for shilling and '**d**' for pence were derived from the Latin solidus and denarius used in the Middle Ages. The '**£**' sign developed from the 'l' for libra.

£ or l in some documents = pound

s or /- = shilling (from the solidus, a Roman coin)

d = penny (from the 'denarius', a Roman coin)

g or gn = guinea

The half-crown was a denomination of British money worth half of a crown, and was the equivalent of two and a half shillings, or one-eighth of a pound. The half-crown coin was first issued in 1549, in the reign of Edward VI.

There were twenty (20) shillings to a pound.

There were twelve (12) pennies to a shilling.

A penny could be sub-divided into two half pennies or four farthings (quarter pennies – which were legal tender right up until 31st December 1960).

2 farthings = 1 halfpenny (ha'penny)

2 halfpennies = 1 penny (1d)

3 pence = 1 thruppence (3d) (a thru'penny bit)

6 pence = 1 sixpence (a 'tanner') (6d)

12 pence = 1 shilling (a bob) (1s)

2 shillings = 1 florin (a 'two bob bit') (2s)

2 shillings and 6 pence = 1 half-crown (2s 6d)

5 shillings = 1 Crown (5s)

The old £1 coin (as opposed to today's £1 coin which is gold in colour) was called a Sovereign and was actually made of gold.

A paper one pound note was and still is often referred to as a 'quid'. There are also five £5, ten £10, twenty £20 and fifty £50 pound notes. In Scotland and Ireland you may even see £100 notes in circulation.

> 1 guinea = £1-1s-0d (£1/1/-) = one pound and one shilling = 21 shillings
>
> (which is £1.05 in today's money)
>
> 1 guinea might be shown on a sign or written as '1g' or '1gn'.

A guinea was considered a more gentlemanly amount than £1. You paid tradesmen, like say a carpenter, in pounds but gentlemen, such as an artist, would typically be paid in guineas.

> A third of a guinea was equal to exactly seven shillings.

Why was it called a guinea? Because the Guinea coast was fabled for its gold, so its name became attached to other things with similarly perceived high value, including but not limited to, the protectorate of British New Guinea in 1884.

NOTES:

Made in the USA
Middletown, DE
08 November 2015